C000172186

"I'm in awe of Peter's encyclopedic and incredibly
Useless hype is stripped away, leaving the inforn
a film-directing treasure trove to be mined with abandon."—**Michael Bruce Adams,
screenwriter; writing instructor, Shanghai Vancouver Film School**

"Peter switched a light on in me and allowed me to say: 'I am a film director.' *Making
the Magic Happen* is like having the best confidant and mentor right there with
you. My bible and all-time favorite 'go-to' book . . . an amazing, all-in-one gift."
—**Jurgen Alan, director**

"Peter blends the knowledge gained in over 40 years in the movie business with his
passion for making good films and enthusiasm for teaching. Invaluable for new
directors, and a great reference for the more experienced . . . should be in every
filmmaker's library." —**Larry D. Barr, director, *88 Days***

"Takes the daunting, scary aspects of directing and tames them with easy-to-follow
checklists . . . forty years of advice, tricks, and life hacks condensed into one book. A
must-read for all directors." —**Jeffrey Michael Bays, producer, *Hitch20***

"Essential . . . a great refresher . . . Peter's straightforward teaching style pulls
back the curtain on the director's process . . . logically outlines the most effective,
efficient ways to translate vision into tangible, collaborative achievement."
—**Darren Borrowman, director, producer, educator**

"Real-world directing advice from the trenches that will save filmmakers time, money,
and heartache. Using plain English and emphasizing how to get the most out of
a script, cast, and crew, Peter's insights on working with others are distinct and
invaluable. Read this book — you'll make better films." —**Dean Burns, screenwriter**

"Bursting with practical information, Peter shows how to conduct yourself as a leader
to get your cinematic story told . . . empowering . . . you *can* jump in and direct by
bringing out the creative best from your cast and crew. Real magic!"
—**Montgomery Burt, screenwriter, producer**

"Featuring Peter's clear, fresh writing, and enriched with anecdotes and real-case
scenarios, *Making the Magic Happen* is the final handbook and ultimate resource on
the craft of film directing. A must if you want a career in film."—**Luis Calandre,
Vice President, Education, Shanghai Vancouver Film School**

"The real deal: a thorough, comprehensive, and detailed description of the role of
the director, broken down with intimate knowledge and authority." —**Lance Carlson,
cinematographer; instructor, George Brown College**

"Engaging . . . a great education. If you're a film geek dreaming of making your own
movies, pick up this book and devour it." —**Kenny Chaplin, assistant director (DGA/
DGC), Film Industry Training Seminars LLC**

"Leaves no stone unturned . . . goes through every step of directing film and television with a fine-tooth comb. As an experienced director, it will teach you things you may have forgotten; as a new director, it's the best roadmap you can get. If you direct, or want to, read this book!" —**Lauro Chartrand, director, writer, stuntman**

"Peter has worked intimately with some of the biggest names in Hollywood. I've learned nearly everything I know about the craft through him, and am delighted to have his lessons in one place . . . should be on all of our shelves." —**Nicholas Humphries, director**

"A brilliant tool for aspiring filmmakers, directors, and visual artists alike, delivering timeless, behind-the-scenes industry information." —**Stephanie Limage, visual artist, filmmaker, digital media marketer, photographer**

"Beyond astounding . . . precise and well-informed, valuable and certainly beneficial . . . Peter is a master of his craft with unlimited passion for helping people succeed. All directors should own *Making the Magic Happen*." —**Sarah Thomas Moffat, Director of Photography, Canadian Society of Cinematographers**

"Teaches you what you really need to know, from the nuts and bolts of directing to getting your movie made and out into the world. An indispensable reference, very insightful . . . easy and fun to read!" —**Dominique Othenin-Girard, independent film director, producer, scriptwriter**

"Focused and practical, each chapter has helpful tips and useful tools that will clarify any director's vision, whether they're students, beginners, or professionals . . . excellent for understanding and organizing all the steps a director takes to bring their story to life." —**John Pozer, director**

"Peter has an incredible understanding of the director/actor relationship and how to nurture and maintain it . . . learn how to build a rapport with your cast that allows for organic, dynamic performances on set. Recommended . . . your career will be long and fruitful if you emulate Peter." —**Rhona Rees, actor, voice artist**

"Peter was the best on-set collaborator I ever had . . . his book is like having his brilliance beside you through every step of the filmmaking process. There's nothing like it." —**Bobby Roth, director**

"From working with actors to planning complex effects sequences and battle scenes, auditioning to post production, documentary to drama, Peter's done it all. This book distills his vast filmmaking knowledge and years on sets around the world into concise, digestible lessons." —**Naim Sutherland, cinematographer**

"Peter's insight and expertise on directing made a HUGE difference in how I approached and executed my first feature film. Without his tips, I would've been lost." —**Michael Thelin, director, *Emelie***

"An entertaining, easy-to-follow, step-by-step filmmaking guide. Filled with advice, explanations, and personal stories from an informed, experienced professional, it's a welcome addition to everyone's filmmaking library." —**Joyce Thierry Llewellyn, story editor, screenwriter**

Making the Magic Happen

THE ART AND CRAFT OF FILM DIRECTING

PETER D. MARSHALL

MICHAEL WIESE PRODUCTIONS

Published by Michael Wiese Productions
12400 Ventura Blvd. #1111
Studio City, CA 91604
(818) 379-8799, (818) 986-3408 (Fax)
mw@mwp.com
www.mwp.com
Manufactured in the United States of America

This book was set in Garamond Premier Pro
and DinPro

Cover design by Johnny Ink. johnnyink.com
Interior design by Debbie Berne
Copyediting by Ross Plotkin

There are no rules in filmmaking. Only opinions.
PETER D. MARSHALL

CONTENTS

ACKNOWLEDGMENTS

I could never have written this book without the love, friendship, and help of the following people who have supported and influenced me in both my personal life and professional life.

I would first like to thank my parents, June and David, and my sisters, Susan, Judy, and Miriam, who always supported my artistic career choice. I want to thank my children, Meghan and Andrew, who helped me grow as a father, who made me laugh during the good times, and who stood by me during the dark times. Tineke Wilders, Kate Pierpoint, and Trilby Jeeves, each one of you has contributed to the person I am today by unconditionally sharing your love, strengths, and vulnerabilities with me. You will forever remain in my heart.

I would like to thank Jim Kelly and Heinz Drega who pointed me in the right direction when I was a film student and to Ralph Bongard who empowered me with the words "Pass it on" when I asked him what I could do to repay him for the trust and guidance he gave me at the start of my career.

I would like to thank the following friends and industry colleagues for their personal and professional friendships: Alex Beaton, Natalie & Wayne Bennet, Pam & Rick Benwick, Bob Burdett, Frank Bush, Lance Carlson, Dawn Leigh Climie, Richard Coleman, Chilton Crane, Mada Dalian, Glenn Davis, Terry Glecoff & Claire Wootten, David Hauka, Roy Hayter & Andrea Oberdieck, Sarah & Sherman Hu, Shiva Kashi, Susan Lambie, William Laurin, Rachel Leiterman, Cindy Lewis, Stephanie Leigh Limage, Karen Margolese, Sandy McGiffert, Mike McLellan, Sarah Thomas Moffat, Robert New, Christopher Penner, Kulwant Rajwans, David Roessell, Bobby Roth, Cindy Smith, Naim Sutherland, Betty Thomas, Mark Travis, Mel Tuck & Karen Austin-Tuck, Ken Wahl, Jaimy Warner, Tiska Wiedermann, Charles Wilkinson, and Aurora Winter.

A special shout-out goes to all the film-industry professionals too numerous to mention here whom I've had the pleasure of working with on some amazing (and not-so-amazing) movies and TV shows.

I would like to give a special mention to all the instructors, students, and staff at the Vancouver Film School, especially Nicholas Humphries, Darren Borrowman, and Steve Belsey.

I would like to give a special mention to all the instructors, students, and staff at the Shanghai Vancouver Film School, especially Elaine Huang, Jenny Mao, Faye Shi, Shawn Tilling, and Alisa Sun.

I would also like to thank the two people who made this book possible, Michael Wiese and Ken Lee of Michael Wiese Productions. The writing of this book is one of the few times I've ever gone over schedule in my career, and I thank you both for your support and understanding.

To Trilby Jeeves, who was with me when I first started to write the eBooks and create the workshops that ultimately became the content for this book — and who finally got me to take her Buffoonery Workshop!

To Michael Bruce Adams, whose friendship I cherish and whose knowledge of films and story structure has enlightened me. You are my secret weapon!

And finally to Che Xioayan. Thank you for smiling at me on that cold and wet Shanghai street corner. I look forward to seeing what the future will bring. (501/2002)

INTRODUCTION

I started making films (on Super 8) when I was 16 years old. I made movies of our high school parties and created pixelated animations with model race cars in my basement.

When I was 18, my parents asked me what I was planning to do when I graduated from high school. After a brief pause, I told them I wanted to be a filmmaker and go to film school.

After a brief pause, they told me they understood my passion but they wanted me to get a general arts degree first before I went to film school. (Sound familiar?)

After a brief pause, I said no. I wanted to go to film school and explained my reasons why. After a brief pause, they said okay, and my parents have forever supported my choice to have a filmmaking career. (Thanks, June and David!)

After graduating from Grade 12 in Regina, Saskatchewan, I moved to Toronto and spent three years in the film program at Ryerson Polytechnical Institute (now a university) from 1970–1973, then hit the streets looking for *the* job that would kick-start my filmmaking career.

Of course, that didn't happen right away! My first paid film job was on a Certs commercial in 1974. I was a production assistant who held a paper bag just under the camera so when the director called "Cut!" the actor could spit the candy into the bag I was holding. Ahh, yes . . . those were the days!

During my 40+ year career, I have worked as a PA, dolly grip, electrician, assistant cameraman, commercial production manager, 1st assistant director, TV series creative consultant, television producer, and director.

My first big directing break came in 1989. I was working as a 1st AD on the TV series *Wiseguy* when the producers gave me a chance to direct two episodes. This happens occasionally on established TV series when actors, producers, writers, DOP's, editors, stunt coordinators, and 1st AD's get an opportunity to direct one or two episodes.

I have directed over 30 episodes of television drama and written, directed, or produced over 50 hours of documentary and educational programs. My documentaries and dramas have won, or been nominated for, 14 international film awards.

As a 1st assistant director, I've worked on 12 Hollywood feature films, 17 television movies, 6 television series, 4 television pilots, and over 20 TV commercials and music videos.

I have worked for directors such as John Woo, Zack Snyder, Phillip Noyce, Mark Rydell, Ed Zwick, John Badham, Roger Vadim, Dennis Dugan, Anne Wheeler, Bobby Roth, and Kim Manners.

I have also worked with such amazing and talented actors as Peter O'Toole, Kevin Spacey, Morgan Freeman, John Travolta, Kathy Bates, Michelle Pfeiffer, Marcia Gay Harden, Madeleine Stowe, Mel Gibson, Ashton Kutcher, Goldie Hawn, Judy Davis, Halle Berry, and Adam Sandler.

I've spent my career in the "trenches" of the film and TV industry. I've had the chance to coordinate huge WWI battle scenes, to plan complicated visual FX scenes, manage large groups of extras, and direct intimate, emotional scenes between actors.

By having this unique opportunity to work as both a television director and a feature-film 1st assistant director, I've been able to get "up close and personal" with major Hollywood studios and TV networks, creative producers, imaginative directors, and Academy Award–winning actors.

During my career, I've been blessed to have worked on dozens of wonderful productions and to have spent quality time with hundreds of very talented and compassionate filmmakers. I've also been able to travel the world making films or teaching fimmaking — and if there is one wonderful result of my career, it's all the fabulous stories I get to tell!

And now I get to share my filmmaking experiences and stories with you!

Peter D. Marshall
May 2017

HOW TO USE THIS BOOK

The 17 chapters in this book follow the actual steps a director goes through during the preproduction, production, and postproduction of any film.

If you are a film student or first-time filmmaker, read each chapter in order (the content of every chapter flows logically into the next one) to get an overview of the film director's logistical and creative role, then start again with Chapter 3 and make notes on each chapter.

If you are an experienced director, but you still get overwhelmed in certain areas (i.e., script analysis, casting and directing actors, blocking for the camera, etc.), you could concentrate on those specific chapters first before going to the beginning of the book and reading each chapter in order.

If you are a film professor, or you teach filmmaking, you can have your students study the specific chapters you are currently teaching in your classroom. You can also use this book to add relevant material to your lectures and workshops.

Chapter 1: Making a film is a stressful job because there is a great deal of money and hundreds of careers on the line every time the camera rolls. In this first chapter, I give you some tools that will help you to work and survive in the "business," as well as sharing the personal philosophy and work ethic to which I will continually refer throughout this book.

Chapter 2: To be a good film director, you need to know the creative and technical filmmaking skills expected when you begin preproduction, when you step on the set, and when you are in the editing room. In this chapter I let you know what is expected of a director by giving you an overview of the film and TV director's main responsibilities.

Chapter 3: The more time you put into preproduction, the more you will discover and organize before you go to camera. This chapter gives a detailed overview of the director's role during the preproduction stage of a film.

Chapter 4: Directors are not only responsible for visually interpreting the script; they also have to be "financially responsible," or you may end up having a very short career! This chapter goes into detail on how to "shoot the schedule" so you have a better chance of finishing your film on time and within budget.

Chapter 5: People are extremely complex; everything we do is influenced by a variety of experiences — from the culture we were born into to our genetic makeup. This chapter gives you an overview of some basic human behaviors that motivate us in our daily lives, and how you can apply these "universal" behaviors to your own stories and films.

Chapter 6: To make a good story idea great, it must be developed properly. In this chapter, we discuss why good drama needs to have characters confront each other. When characters are in conflict, the audience experiences this conflict and is drawn into the story.

Chapter 7: The best story structure persuades an audience to feel that the story is organic and authentic. This chapter shows you why human beings universally understand story best in one way: within a problem-solving three-act structure. The further we move away from that structure, the less engaging our films will be.

Chapter 8: To be a good storyteller a director needs to first understand every detail about the story they are telling. In this chapter, I explain how to break down a script and analyze each scene to discover what the story is really about; what the main theme is; what the story points are; who the main characters are; and what happens to them.

Chapter 9: To find the "heartbeat" of any script, a director needs to understand the "sub-world" of the characters. This chapter shows you how to perform detailed analysis of every character to discover their backstory, scene objectives, internal and external traits, strengths and weaknesses, and their relationships to the other characters.

Chapter 10: The *15-Step Scene Breakdown System* is a tool I use to analyze any script. It takes the most important story and scene elements discussed in this book and organizes them into an easy-to-follow format that takes much of the guess-work out of your script and scene breakdown process.

Chapter 11: Before you can fully bring any script to life, you need to first immerse yourself in the film's story world. This chapter discusses how to research different sources to create the director's visual concept, which is your visual approach to the plot and themes of the film.

Chapter 12: For many directors, working with experienced actors can be very frustrating, and if an actor and director do not connect creatively or personally, performances could suffer. In this chapter I discuss key acting words and phrases that will help you direct actors in a language they understand.

Chapter 13: If you are a student filmmaker or a low-budget indie director, how do you find the best actors for your project when you are not able to attract (or pay) for the most experienced talent? In this chapter, I show you how to discover talented actors who could be right for a part in your film — as long as you know how to attract them to your audition.

Chapter 14: The casting session can be an intimidating experience for both actors and directors because it's where "both sides of the table" have only a few minutes to make creative choices that could affect everybody's careers! Since there is never enough time to work with actors during an audition, in this chapter I will focus on the top three qualities you should concentrate on in casting.

Chapter 15: When you first start directing, blocking actors can be one of the most difficult parts of your job. Get it wrong here and you could waste valuable time on set! In this chapter I discuss the specific blocking strategy I use that leads to motivated actor movement and creates organic and believable performances.

Chapter 16: Every director needs to understand the various camera techniques that can enhance the visual storytelling power of their film. In this chapter I discuss the "language of the camera." The better you can communicate a technical detail to the crew, the better chance you have of getting it!

Chapter 17: Every film goes through different postproduction stages based on the complexity of the story elements (action, visual effects) and how much editing time (budget) was scheduled. In this chapter I walk you through the director's role during postproduction — from viewing dailies to color correction.

DEMYSTIFYING THE FILM-DIRECTING PROCESS

MY MISSION

I remember getting an email from an indie fimmaker who was a subscriber to my monthly online ezine *The Director's Chair.* He told me that the information I wrote about in the ezine was clear and easy to understand, and that I'd helped to "demystify" the filmmaking process for him.

That email forever changed the way I thought about my role as a filmmaker and educator. From that day on, I made it my goal (my "mission") to help demystify the film-directing process for filmmakers worldwide.

No matter how many years of experience your cast and crew have, or the size of your budget, making any kind of film is a complicated and risky venture. All films have at least one thing in common: a lot of "moving pieces"! And if even one of those pieces is out of sync with the rest, problems will begin to appear.

Every film you make will have its own challenges, but directing a movie is actually less complicated than you think. The trick is to learn the "craft" of filmmaking first, and then adapt your personal skills and creative ability to the "art" of filmmaking. In other words, there is an "art and craft" to making movies. **Learn the craft first — then perfect your art!**

STORY, PERFORMANCE, CINEMATICS

"Making a (good) movie is the *art* of *visually* telling a *compelling* story with *believable* characters who make us *feel* something."

If you agree with my definition of making a good movie, how DO you make a film that has a compelling story with believable characters who make us feel something?

Many scriptwriters, directors, producers, studios, etc. have tried to find a winning formula for making a successful movie by copying films that have worked in the past. Some of these films have been successful — most have not.

But making a "successful" film depends on your definition of success. You must first decide what "a successful film" means to you: Did the audiences love it? Did the critics love it? Did it win awards? Did it make money?

During my career, I've had the opportunity to work on many different types of productions, from industrial films to documentaries, television commercials to music videos, Emmy Award–nominated TV series to Hollywood feature films.

I've worked with dozens of directors and hundreds of actors, varying from the great and the good to the bad. I've read hundreds of film scripts, some of which were so dreadful I couldn't get past the first 10 pages to some that hooked me from page one and went on to win Academy Awards.

As a film-directing coach, I've spent countless hours mentoring filmmakers around the world — from showing them how to conduct proper script analysis to helping them effectively direct actors during an audition.

I've also had the incredible opportunity of spending years teaching and mentoring hundreds of film students as they write, prep, shoot, and edit their short films.

> As I write this book, I'm living in China and working as the directing instructor at the Shanghai Vancouver Film School. Combined with over 8 years as a directing instructor at the Vancouver Film School, I've mentored hundreds of international film students through the preproduction, production, or postproduction phases of over *500 short films*, giving me great insight into the art and craft of good filmmaking!

All the years I've spent in the "professional film-production trenches," plus all the years I've been teaching filmmakers around the world, have given me a unique insight into finding an answer to the question:

"Is there a simple guide that directors anywhere can follow to help them demystify and better understand the craft of filmmaking?"

We all know there's no 100% guarantee of anything being successful in our business, but I believe I have found a basic approach that any filmmaker can follow to help them create "compelling movies with believable characters."

Most inexperienced (or lazy) directors spend the majority of their time figuring out how to shoot their films first (cool visual effects, creative shots and camera angles, etc.) before they understand: a) what their story is really about; and b) what their characters really want. And from what I have witnessed over the years, this is not the best way to make a good film!

Why? Because I strongly believe that to successfully direct a "visually compelling story with believable characters," you should follow (in order) this 3-step film-directing guide: "Story — Performance — Cinematics!"

Story: The first and most important part of a director's job is to understand every detail of the story he or she is about to tell. This requires you to dig deep into the story and its structure by analyzing each individual scene in the script to find out what it is about, what works, and what doesn't.

Performance: One of the main responsibilities of a director is to help actors achieve a realistic performance. Actors want to work with directors who understand their vulnerabilities, so it's incredibly important to create a good relationship with every actor in your film — right from the first audition!

Cinematics (Mise-en-Scène): Originating from the theater, the French term mise-en-scène literally means "putting on the stage." In cinema, mise-en-scène refers to everything that is shown in front of the camera: sets, props, actors, costumes, lighting, etc.

Without understanding these 3 steps, you set yourself up for "filmmaker mediocrity": writing unimaginative scripts with *unbelievable* characters that create *boring* and *predictable* films.

As a visual storyteller you must always listen to your heart so your camera can show us your version of life and art. If you follow this 3-step film-directing guide, you will see how any director, even someone with very little experience, has the potential to create a **visually compelling movie with believable characters**.

The rest of this book expands this 3-step guide by demystifying the film-directing process step by step so you can better understand the art and craft of filmmaking.

1

THE TEN COMMANDMENTS
OF FILMMAKING

One of the great things about being a director as a life choice is that it can never be mastered. Every story is its own kind of expedition, with its own set of challenges. —RON HOWARD

THE TEN COMMANDMENTS OF FILMMAKING

All my years in the film and TV business has taught me many lessons, but the main lesson I have learned is to "remain human at all costs." And by this I mean to simply "treat others as you would like to be treated yourself."

Making a film is a stressful job because there is a great deal of money and hundreds of careers on the line every time the camera rolls. This is a business of artistic expression, massive egos, and huge amounts of cash, a recipe for disaster if I ever saw one! It's also a business where you could lose your soul if you're not careful.

With that in mind, I created the following "Ten Commandments of Filmmaking," my way of demonstrating how anyone can (and should) work and survive in this business without getting OR giving ulcers! This list also gives you some insight into my personal philosophy and work ethic.

COMMANDMENT 1 It's only a movie — no one should get hurt

This one should be obvious. Making any kind of film or TV production can be risky because there are so many natural hazards on a film set: Crew members can trip over cables or fall off platforms; equipment can tumble onto the cast; performers can burn and cut themselves or slip down stairs.

Then there are the added hazards specific to our industry: breathing atmosphere smoke for long periods, accidents involving insert cars or process trailers,

1

mishaps involving stunts and special effects, and noise hazards such as loud explosions and gunfire.

All crew members should be aware of the safety issues of working on any set. If you have any concerns or suggestions, talk to your shop steward, union representative, or the 1st assistant director who is, on most productions around the world, the set safety supervisor.

COMMANDMENT 2 **Ask lots of questions and never assume anything**
Don't be afraid to ask questions. Indeed, the only dumb question is the one that was never asked. As a director, you have to answer questions all day, but you also have to ask questions. If something doesn't feel right, or doesn't make sense, ask questions. Solve it now!

Assuming that everything will be "ready on the day" is wrong thinking. If something in the script doesn't make sense, or you feel something is not working, deal with it right away. Because if it doesn't work in the script, it sure won't work on set.

> This attitude of "it will be alright when we shoot" will come back and haunt you 9 times out of 10. And by the way, you can't always "fix it in post"!

Never assume anything. Never! Fix it, change it, eliminate it, solve it, get rid of it. Whatever IT is, do something about it *before* you go to camera.

COMMANDMENT 3 **There are no rules in filmmaking — only opinions!**
Everyone you work with on a movie will have an opinion about something. That can be a good thing. It can also be a bad thing.

Don't get overwhelmed with all the opinions and suggestions you will hear each day. Listen to everyone, evaluate their ideas, and then make your decisions. You will always second-guess yourself. It takes time and experience to trust your own instincts as much as you do others.

COMMANDMENT 4 **Listen to the people who know more than you do**
Film crews work on the set all the time! That's what they do for a living. They see directors come and go. Experienced crew members will usually know more "set stuff" than you do and their help can be invaluable. So if you want to become a better filmmaker, listen to them!

COMMANDMENT 5   **You have to EARN respect — not demand it**
The hierarchy of a movie is like a military hierarchy: generals at the top and privates at the bottom. And just like the military, there are certain people in higher positions that you won't like or will be unable to get along with.

Directors, 1st AD's, and DOP's form the "triumvirate" of any movie set. They are the people in charge; many times you will be faced with the difficult task of working for weeks or months with people who are egotistical, abusive, or sometimes incompetent at their job.

The majority of cast or crew who "act up" on set are just *insecure*. They work in a position of authority in a creative environment, so they feel they are "allowed" to have temper tantrums and yell at people.

This will always happen. How I deal with this situation (and I suggest you do the same) is to remember the military expression: "Respect the rank. You don't have to like the person."

COMMANDMENT 6   **Don't abuse your power. Use "power through," not "power over"**
Directors have a very powerful position in the film industry. Producers look to you to make sure the movie comes in on time and on budget; the crew looks to you for leadership; and the cast looks to you for vision, support, and empathy.

The "rank" of director means you carry "a big stick," but there are many directors who abuse this power and make everyone's life miserable by taking advantage of their position and using their power *over* people.

> Now here's a good idea . . . let's yell and scream at everyone, and they'll work harder! NOT! (I remember a dolly grip who said to me early in my AD career, when I was trying to rush the crew to get a shot, "If you don't like this speed, you're going to hate the next one." I got the message!)

My philosophy is to take the other route and use "power through" by bringing your crew together as a team and working it out together. The crew knows you are in charge. You don't have to keep advertising it.

COMMANDMENT 7   **Don't be afraid to change your mind**
I read a self-help book that also had a set of ten commandments, and one of them was: "It's okay to change your mind."

This makes a lot of sense, especially when you are a director or 1st AD, because you're making decisions all the time. Some of your decisions may need to change after you get more information from other people, but problems could occur if your ego gets in the way.

I did that once as a 1st AD. I thought I had a good schedule and I didn't listen to the director and PM, who both thought we couldn't make the day. Well . . . we didn't make our day, and I cost the production money, all because I didn't want to change my decision for fear that others would feel I didn't know what I was doing (which turned out to be correct in this instance anyway). Lesson learned!

COMMANDMENT 8   **Self-confidence is necessary — self-importance is unnecessary**

Ego can be defined as "your consciousness of your own identity." You need an ego in this business because ego is important for your survival. But there is an important distinction between the two types of ego: *self-confidence* and *self-importance*.

Self-confidence (good ego) helps you believe in yourself and get up in the morning knowing that you are good at your job, but still have things to learn. You will get through your day by being fair and respecting others.

On the other hand, *self-importance* (misplaced ego) is "an inflated feeling of pride in your superiority to others." I believe it's this trait, more than anything else, that makes working and surviving in the film industry harder than it has to be.

COMMANDMENT 9   **Have a sense of humor and learn to laugh at yourself**

This rule should probably be #1 on this list. In my experience, the best film sets are the ones that have a relaxed and professional atmosphere presided over by a creative director with no insecurity issues, an experienced 1st AD with no attitude problems, and a DOP who realizes that making a film is not all about the lighting!

Making a movie is hard work, but it can also be fun, and the occasional break from the stress of the set by having a laugh pays for itself many times over.

I've found that my sense of humor (and my large repertoire of bad jokes and puns) have gotten me through some very difficult times. I also think it is important to feel that you can say to the crew, "I don't care whether you laugh with me, at me, or about me — as long as you laugh!"

COMMANDMENT 10   **Take 10 at lunch to change your shoes and socks**

Yes, I am serious! Taking a moment after lunch to change your socks and shoes is a blissful moment — it actually reenergizes you. There's probably some psychological or chemical reason for this. Try it.

I like to have about 15 minutes on my own during lunch to have a quiet time to "recharge my batteries." As a director, you have to be on your game all day and make hundreds of decisions with the cast and crew constantly asking you questions. Taking some time for yourself is really, really important to keep your body relaxed and your mind sharp.

2

THE WORKING FILM DIRECTOR

The prospect of directing a film is overwhelming. Not only is it not very clear or even agreed upon as to what a director does, but there are very few guidelines or programs for the learning director. There is no particular structure or manual that comes along with the job. —MARK TRAVIS*

WHAT IS EXPECTED OF A DIRECTOR?

Directing a film is not only about visually interpreting the screenplay and creatively handling actors; it also includes the ability to complete a day's work on time and on schedule.

courtesy Mehtap Kizilirmak

Like any artist, a good director understands the necessity of working from the "inside out." In other words, a good director needs to work on him/herself first so they can develop the artistic, logistic, and emotional skills that will enable them to see and hear "the truth" in their work.

To be a good film director, you also need to know the creative and technical filmmaking skills that are expected of you when you begin preproduction, step onto the set, and tackle the editing room.

Ultimately, I believe the director's main job is to *empower* their cast and crew to work creatively and collaboratively with

Directing Feature Films: The Creative Collaboration Between Director, Writers, and Actors (Michael Wiese Productions, 2002)

6

one firm goal in mind: to make the best film they can within their budgetary and time constraints.

WHAT ARE THE DIRECTOR'S RESPONSIBILITIES?

Here's a useful description from the Directors Guild of Canada (DGC)[*] to give you an idea of what a film and television director's responsibilities are:

(a) The director is engaged by the producer and assigned by the producer to direct a motion picture. The director directs whatever is seen and heard in a motion picture. The director has the right to be present on the set whenever shooting is in progress. The fact that the director may also render services as producer or writer or in any other capacity shall not change the director's job classification, with reference to work performed as a director, and during the period of such work.

(b) The terms "director" and "directing" as used herein shall include directing all related functions and activities required for translating and transferring the premise, idea, and/or concept to the audiovisual images.

(c) A director's duties include the following: Survey and approve all locations and their use as they pertain to the directorial idea and need; directorial planning and breakdown of the shooting script; plot the camera angle and compositions within the frame; participate in determining the requirements of the set, costumes, makeup, props, etc., for their proper directorial perspective and mechanical functioning; participate in the final casting of all performers; rehearse actors, extras, and any of the visual and audio devices necessary for the completion of the production; direct the action of all performers, extras, etc.; direct the dialogue as well as prerecording and post-recording of dialogue; directly supervise the duties of the entire crew during the rehearsal and shooting periods; make such script changes as necessary, within the director's jurisdiction, for the proper audiovisual presentation of the production; the right to the "first cut."

(d) The director's total function is to contribute creatively to all the above elements and to guide, mold, and integrate them into one cohesive, dramatic, and aesthetic whole.

---

[*]Reprinted with permission from the Directors Guild of Canada, Toronto, Ontario.

FIVE TYPES OF DIRECTORS

What kind of person becomes a director? What kind of experience do they need to have? Do they have to go to film school? Should they have industry experience in another crew position?

There are very few rules when it comes to declaring yourself a director because everyone's background and circumstances are unique. What may work for one person may not (and probably won't) work for another.

Directors can come from a creative background (writer, actor) or from a production background (DOP, editor). They can learn their trade by going to film school or from shooting films on their own. But no matter what a director's background or education, here are the "five types" of directors I think we all fit into. Which type of director are you — right now?

Newbie (Film School) Director

This director is usually a young film student who is just learning the filmmaking process. They only have a basic (mostly theoretical) knowledge of how a film is made, and they have had very little practical "on-set" time working with actors or the camera.

Newbie (Film Professional) Director

This director is someone who has some film-production experience in another crew position who has been given a chance to direct. They may have years of experience in that position but very little (or no) experience as a director (i.e., a producer, writer, 1st AD, editor, actor, DOP, or stunt coordinator).

Skilled (Technical) Director

This is an experienced director who focuses primarily on the technical aspects of the shot and scene with the crew. This director spends very little time giving direction to actors. They may just "let the actors do their thing," or they may not know how to communicate with the talent.

Skilled (Performance) Director

This is an experienced director who understands the story and can get good performances from actors, but only has a basic knowledge of the technical aspects of filmmaking such as blocking, composition, camera placement, lens sizes, etc.

Skilled (Art & Craft) Director

This is an individual who is the perfect combination of the "performance" director and the "technical" director. They understand the actor and the acting process; they know how to work with the crew; they understand the editing process; and they know the technical aspects of film production well enough to communicate effectively with everybody.

> Did you know that the director is the only department head on a movie that doesn't need any experience — and the film will still get made? (I'm not joking. I've seen this happen too many times to be funny!)

HOW TO WORK AND SURVIVE IN THE "BUSINESS"

I believe that to be successful in this business, you need to fully understand the *business* of film; the *politics* of film; the *power players* in film (and how to deal with them); and the *differences* between film and television.

> Here is the major difference between working on a feature film and on a television series: television is a producer's medium, and feature film is a director's medium. This fact alone will give you a distinct advantage when it comes to surviving in the film and TV industry!

Here are 10 tips to *have*, *learn*, or *nurture* for working and surviving in today's film and television business:

1. You need film-set *experience*. (Make short films; go to film school; work for free.)
2. You need to make your own *luck*. (This means being at the right place at the right time.)
3. You need to find, make, and nurture industry *connections*. (This is a "who you know" business.)
4. You need to have *determination*. (You must always believe in yourself.)
5. You have to tap into your *creativity*. (We are all born with a special gift. What's yours?)

6. You need to know how to *market and promote* yourself. (To continue making movies for a living, you must treat it like a business.)
7. You need to understand the *unspoken rules* of the film world. (These are the universal film-industry politics.)
8. You have to *earn* the respect of the cast and crew. (You cannot demand it.)
9. You need to *listen* to everyone. (Especially those who know more than you.)
10. You need to have *PASSION*! (Because some days that may be the only thing that will keep you going.)

THE WORKING FILM DIRECTOR

Charles Wilkinson is a director who lives in Vancouver, Canada. He has written a book called *The Working Film Director** that is not about the great masters of cinema or where to place the camera. He has written a book about how to get hired to direct film and television projects again and again!

I strongly recommend you get this book. It will save you years of struggle and frustration because it does what so many other film books fail to do: elucidate the business and politics of the film and television industry.

You're up against serious competition for every directing job, and there are things you do or neglect to do every day that affect your chances of being hired. From that all-important first phone call through prep, production, and post, right up to getting your next and better job, Charles tells you how to get the job, do it well, and make the friends who will hire you to do the job again.

---

*Charles Wilkinson, *The Working Film Director: How to Arrive, Survive & Thrive in the Director's Chair* (Michael Wiese Productions, 2nd edition, 2013)

3

DIRECTING THE PREPRODUCTION

A great movie evolves when everybody has the same vision in their heads. —ALAN PARKER

THE REDUCTIONISM BREAKDOWN SYSTEM

Here is my simplified analysis of reductionism: "Most anything can be understood by taking its pieces apart, studying them, and then putting them back together so you can see the larger picture."

For our purposes as filmmakers, we use the *reductionism breakdown system* as "the process of reducing a script down to its smallest individual elements by going from large to small, from general to specific."

> Every department on a movie uses this breakdown system: The producer to create budgets; the director for script analysis and shot lists; the 1st AD to create the shooting schedule, etc.

Here's an example of the director's reductionism breakdown system order from the first reading of a script through the first shot on set: *Script — Act — Sequence — Scene — Shot — Take.*

I have a very good personal example of the reductionism breakdown system. When I got the job as 1st assistant director on *Bird on a Wire*, I was overwhelmed by the creative and technical logistics of this big action comedy. Plus I was a little nervous working with a director as established as John Badham.

I honestly wondered how I could possibly prepare such a demanding show with two major Hollywood stars (Mel Gibson and Goldie Hawn), lots of stunt action, and many locations spread over two cities. But after two months of prep, I was totally ready for our first day of shooting!

I had been overwhelmed by my first script read-through because I only saw the magnitude of the film as a whole. I was just looking ahead to the end result — with no idea of how to get there! But once I started to reduce it into more manageable elements, it became clearer and clearer each day how to proceed.

THE DIRECTOR'S PREPRODUCTION ACTIVITIES

The following list is a detailed overview of what is expected of a director during preproduction, the most important time for a director because it's actually a "*process of discovery.*"

It's also during this time that every department discovers what they need to make a particular movie. All this takes time. The more time you have in prep, the more you will discover and sort out before you go to camera.

Please keep in mind that these preproduction activities will vary in time and importance depending on whether you are shooting a (no-money) short film, a (low-budget/high-budget) feature film, or an episode of a television series.

Before the Cast Arrives
1. Director's Visual Concept
2. Creative Concept Meeting
3. Script Meetings (Ongoing)
4. Key Crew Interviews & Hiring
5. Script Analysis
6. Location Scouts (Ongoing)
7. Department Head Meetings (Ongoing)
8. Budget Meetings (Producers/PM)
9. Shot Lists, Storyboards, Schematics (Ongoing)
10. Casting and Callbacks (Ongoing)
11. Second Unit Meetings
12. Key Location Survey
13. Production Meeting

After the Cast Arrives
14. Actor Meetings
15. Script Read-Through

16. Cast Rehearsals
17. Wardrobe Fittings
18. Props Show-and-Tell
19. Art Department Meetings
20. Special Training and Rehearsals
21. Hair, Makeup, and Costume Camera Tests
22. Camera & Lighting Tests
23. Pre-Shoots

BEFORE THE CAST ARRIVES

1. Director's Visual Concept

The French term *mise-en-scène* literally means "putting on stage." In cinema, mise-en-scène refers to everything that appears before the camera: sets, props, actors, costumes, lighting, blocking, etc.

The *sub-world* of a film means all the feelings and sensations a director creates to arouse certain emotions from the audience. To do this, the director directs the story "beneath" the main story by developing actions, events, and incidents that portray the deeper meaning of the story and the subtext of the characters.

The director's *visual concept* is how he or she creates the image structure and style of the film — it's the "visual stamp" or look they put on the picture. Some examples of visual style are:

- Deciding on what the audience is going to see (and not see) by deciding where to place the camera.
- What is the pacing and mood of the story? (Fast or slow; dark and moody or light and fun?)
- What is the rhythm of the story (or the scene, or the act)? (Every scene should have highs and lows.)
- What is the color of the story? (Colors can be used to express feelings and emotions and to represent certain qualities of a character that can affect the sets and the costumes.)

2. Creative Concept Meetings

The *"producer" concept meeting* is usually one of the first meetings a director has after being hired for a project. It's where you have a chance to communicate your creative ideas, the tone of the film, and your overall vision of the story to the producers.

You will also have several *"key creative" concept meetings* during prep with your key department heads (DOP, production designer, costume designer, etc.) These meetings give them a chance to get a first impression of you, to know your personal style, and to find out if you are organized and well prepared.

3. Script Meetings (Ongoing)

In script meetings you discuss your script notes with the producers and writers. They generally happen after you have had some time to do a basic scene analysis of the script.

Your script breakdown will be a never-ending process, so you will usually have several more script-revision meetings during prep to discuss the variety of script changes that happen before shooting: changes to locations, changes in budget, changes to the cast, changes for script length, etc.

4. Key Crew Interviews & Hiring

As the director you will want to participate in the hiring of your *key creatives* to make sure they are the right fit for you and the film. Depending on the budget of your film, the main key "production" creatives you want to interview and hire (with the producers) are the DOP, production designer, 1st AD, costume designer, key makeup, key hair, prop master, stunt coordinator, script supervisor, and visual-effects supervisor.

The main "key postproduction creatives" you want to interview and hire (with the producers) are the postproduction supervisor, editor, and music composer.

5. Script Analysis

Script and Scene Analysis

When you begin the script-analysis process, your *first impressions* are vital. Keep in mind your emotional reaction to the story and what images the story stimulates in you. What you "feel" when you read the script is really what counts, because it is your emotional response to something that usually defines it as a "truth."

Character Analysis

After reading the script and making notes about script structure and scene analysis, the director needs to figure out the objectives of the characters. You do this by understanding the characters' backgrounds, objectives, and dialogue.

To understand the script deeply, you need to operate in the sub-world of the characters; therefore, one of the main purposes of script analysis is for you to find out who the characters are and what happens to them.

6. Location Scouts (Ongoing)

Location scouting is one of the first preproduction activities. Once a director has had his/her concept meeting with the producers and the key creative team, and they know what kind of look you require for the film, the search for suitable locations begins.

The location manager has a concept meeting with the producer, director, and production designer after reading the script. The location manager finds as many choices as possible for the director, and the creative team then goes on the scout.

Who usually goes on location scouts? Producer, director, location manager, 1st assistant director, production manager or unit production manager, production designer or art director, transportation captain or driver.

One of the biggest challenges when looking for a great location is you have to think "will it work logistically for the shooting schedule?" The main factors that eventually determine if you can get a particular location (after you know it fits the story) are cost, sound issues, power availability, and logistics.

I have divided scouts into two sections based on time and budget:

First Scouts (When you have lots of time)

- Does the location work for the director?
- Does it work for the schedule?

Last Scouts (When you have no time left)

- Does the location work for the schedule?
- Does it work for the director?

7. Department-Head Meetings (Ongoing)

Department-head meetings range from script and concept meetings with the producers to individual department-head meetings. For every element you have in your film, you need to have several meetings with the department head to discuss all the creative and logistical requirements of every scene including those elements.

Depending on your budget and the complexity of the film, you could have more (or fewer) department-head meetings than these.

- Producers (Concept meeting/cast and show info)
- Producers/Writer (Script notes/dialogue changes)
- Location Manager (Location choices, choices, and more choices)
- First Assistant Director (Shooting schedule, shot lists, scene timings)
- Director of Photography (Photographic style, shot lists, lenses)
- Production Designer (Locations and set design)
- Set Decorator (The dressing, look, and feel of the set)
- Costume Designer (Photos, drawings, fabric)
- Hair and Makeup (Various styles, beauty, aging, prosthetics)
- Props Master (Anything an actor touches is a prop)
- Sound Mixer (Music playback, overlapping dialogue)
- Special-Effects Coordinator (Explosion/smoke/squibs/special devices)
- Stunt Coordinator (Actor action/stunt doubles/fights and action sequences)
- Extras Casting (1AD, 2AD, extras casting, costume designer go over extras for the show to decide how many extras/the specific look)
- Transportation Coordinator (Planes, trains, boats, automobiles)
- Visual-Effects Supervisor (CGI/green screen/crowd duplication)
- Animal Trainers
  Domestic Animals (cats, dogs, birds, snakes)
  Exotic Animals (tigers, alligators, monkeys)
  Livestock Wrangler (horses, cows, oxen, wagons)
- Stock Shots, Photographs, Inserts
  Make sure your 1st AD makes a note of all of these items with the appropriate departments so nothing is forgotten.
- Video Playback and Computer Playback
  Video playback is used for scenes that require an image on a television monitor to be viewed by the camera on set. Computer playback is when the camera sees images on a computer screen on set.

The 1st AD needs to make note of all the scenes that require playback and when they occur in the one-liner so they can schedule enough time before these scenes are shot for the TV playback images and for computer images to be created.

- Production Coordinator

  I want to give special mention here to the office production coordinator. I call them (and their staff) the "unsung heroes" of the production. The production office handles all the paperwork distribution, script revisions, travel memos, crew lists, prep lunches, and just about everything else that makes a film shoot run smoothly and efficiently.

  They are usually one of the first people you meet when you get to the production office, and the PC and his or her staff will help you with everything from ordering lunches to getting a stapler to arranging your travel.

8. Budget Meetings (Producers/PM)

A budget is typically divided into four sections: above the line (creative talent in front and behind the camera), below the line (direct production costs and crew costs), postproduction (editing, sound design, visual effects), and other (completion bonds, insurance, contingencies).

The director needs to understand how to read a budget to know where elements can be added or taken away. You will also have to sign off on the budget for legal reasons to ensure that the shoot won't exceed the number of approved shooting days and will operate within the approved budget.

9. Shot Lists, Storyboards, Schematics

Shot Lists

A shot list is a description of all the camera angles for a scene and can include shot size, camera movement, character movement, coverage, and cutaways.

Creating an accurate shot list is useful for several reasons: it helps you understand the flow of each scene and how it connects with other scenes; it guides you through the rehearsal stage and the on-set blocking process; it gives the 1st AD an idea of how many shots/setups you have per scene to help them create a better schedule; and it helps the DOP know your shooting style and potential coverage.

A shot list is like a roadmap: it gives you a path to your destination, but you don't always have to follow it. Changes will happen on set, so you will want to always use your shot list as a good guide.

Like most things in the film business, there is no standard format
to follow to help you write a shot list. It varies from director to
director. Many directors do not make shot lists — at least they don't
show it to anyone on set (unlike most TV commercial directors, who
have to work with shot lists AND storyboards).

Storyboards

A storyboard is a series of illustrations or images used to previsualize certain scenes
in a movie. Some directors will want to storyboard the entire movie, but most storyboard sequences are created just for complicated action scenes or visual-effects
sequences.

Schematics

A schematic is a top-level-view diagram of how the director wants to block a
scene, showing where the actors will move and where the camera positions will
be placed for coverage.

10. Casting and Callbacks

When a director first starts prep, they read the script several times to get a feel for
what the story is about and who the characters are. They then have a meeting with
the producers and casting director to discuss their ideas of the characters. After
this meeting, the casting director puts together a list of actors that fit the character traits and specific looks discussed in the meeting with the producers.

The casting director then has her/his own casting session where they record a
"short list" of actors for the director and the producers to view. After the producer
and director have chosen the actors they want to audition, casting sessions and
callbacks are set up and the actors are chosen.

11. Second Unit Meetings

Second units are smaller film-production units that work on specific scenes during
the main unit shooting period. They usually handle visual-effect plate shots, stunt
scenes (car chases with stunt doubles), aerial shots, establishing shots, and insert
shots. They can even film entire dialogue scenes with actors if the main unit cannot find the time to shoot them.

Some TV series have full-time second units that act as "clean-up crews";
they tend to shoot material for scenes the main unit couldn't get, as well as
reshoot scenes from previous episodes. (I like to refer to main unit as "shooting

from the neck up" and second unit as "shooting from the neck down.")

The following activities are usually done in the last few days (or last few weeks) of preproduction, depending on your budget.

12. Key Location Survey

The key location survey is where the producers and director plus the department heads and their assistants visit all the locations for the film. This gives the shooting crew one more chance to go over all the technical and logistical requirements for filming at a particular location. Depending on how many locations you have and the budget of your film, this survey could take a half day or several days.

From the director's point of view, this survey is not about explaining every shot. It's about discussing where the camera will be looking, what the lighting requirements are, what the art department specifics are, where the work trucks can park, and other technical concerns such as sound, stunts, and special effects.

Who goes on the key location survey: Director, 1AD, 2AD, PM, LM, ALM, producers, set dec, production designer, art director, DOP, grip, gaffer, transportation captain, construction coordinator, sound mixer, stunts, special FX, visual FX. (Depending on the complexity of the film, this survey might have more or less crew.)

13. Production Meeting

The production meeting is an open discussion about the show. All the department heads (and their seconds) need to be at this final meeting to review the director's creative concepts, film-production elements, and specific production logistics.

The 1st AD reads the script scene by scene (no dialogue) so every department can discuss their specific requirements with the director. After the script is read, the 1st AD goes over the one-liner and shooting schedule to discuss each shooting day.

Sidebar Meetings: If certain departments need more time to discuss their specific scene requirements with the director, the 1st AD schedules these smaller meetings after the production meeting.

AFTER THE CAST ARRIVES

Once you have completed your tech survey and production meeting, the main actors will arrive from out of town or (if local) come to the production office during the last week of preproduction. This is the time when the actors go through a series of meetings, fittings, rehearsals, and tests.

14. Actor Meetings

Informal meetings and dinners are a great way to get to know your actors personally, and they really help to strengthen the trust bond between the director and the actor.

15. Script Read-Through

The script read-through (or table read) is when the director, producers, and writer sit around a table with all the available cast and read the script scene by scene to see how it flows and "sounds." They discuss the story and characters, and address script problems such as dialogue concerns, character motivations, scene length, etc.

This read-through is the first opportunity for all the creatives to get together and rework the script based on the actors' suggestions. If the whole cast cannot be present, two other actors (one male and one female) are usually hired to read the other parts. (If you have a small budget, the producers can read the other parts.)

Other key crew members usually present are the DOP, 1st AD, and the script supervisor. Not only do these key crew members get to meet the actors in an informal setting, but everyone around the table gets a sense of how they will all work together for the next few weeks or months.

16. Cast Rehearsals

> The goals of rehearsal are first, to make sure the actors listen and work honestly, use themselves, and find some authentic connection to the material; second, investigate the text: that is, explore questions, problems, and possible meanings of individual lines, and solve the structure of the scene (events, through-lines, and beats); third, block the scene and find the physical life; fourth, established the actor-director relationship, set up your system of communication, hear and try the actors' ideas, and smoke out their resistances. —JUDITH WESTON, *Directing Actors: Creating Memorable Performances for Film & Television* (Michael Wiese Productions, 1996)

After the script read-through, rehearse as many scenes as possible with the actors based on your specific needs and actor requests so you can sort out character concerns and story issues privately before standing on a set with 25 crew members watching.

Most of these rehearsals take place in large rooms, but sometimes they can take place on the actual sets or real locations that are going to be used in the film. Again, it is all based on how much time and money you have.

> At some point you are going to run out of time during your last week of prep, so these cast rehearsals usually happen on the weekend before you start shooting.

17. Wardrobe Fittings

The costume designer needs time to find the right wardrobe for the actors based on the early concept meetings with the director and producer. This process gets more complicated if your film is a period piece or if the costume department must "build" (design and make) the costumes.

The costume designer will never find or make all the costumes for the entire show before you go to camera. Like all departments during this last week of prep, the costume designer will only fit the costumes based on the latest shooting schedule.

18. Props Show-and-Tell

Actors will need a variety of props during a shoot. In this meeting, the prop department presents possible props for approval from the director and actors. There are also actor measurements for proper ring, clothing, and accessory sizes.

19. Art Department Meetings

Depending on the subject matter and the time period of your film, the art department will need to get personal photos from the actors, as well as shoot photos of them "in character," to sell the environments in which they live. For example, when an actor walks into her "home" on the set, you will want to see photos of her and her "family."

And what about when a cop shows his police ID photograph, or we see a mug shot of a "bad guy"? These photographs have to be taken by the props department before the scene takes place.

20. Special Training and Rehearsals

Do the actors in your film have to ballroom dance? Swordfight? Shoot weapons? Drive a certain vehicle? Be part of an special unit like a soldier, cop, firefighter? Speak with a dialect?

This last week of prep is also the time when actors are given the opportunity for special training and rehearsals. A character in a film knows what they are doing in their chosen profession but the actor may not, so it is imperative that the actors get as much training and rehearsal time as possible throughout the film.

21. Hair, Makeup, and Costume Camera Tests

Actor hair and makeup tests are essential at this time as well. The relationship between the actors and the DOP is a very important one because the actors want to know how they will look in front of the camera. (Many a DOP has been fired after a few days of shooting because of this fact alone!)

Special make-up effects need to be tested for color and texture, as well as the "filmic" look of specific hair designs and wigs. These camera tests are also important for studio and network executives who want to see what they'll be getting for their money.

22. Technical Camera Tests and Lighting Tests

Technical camera tests are very important for both the DOP and director because they give them a good idea of what the film "will look like" before they go to camera. Lenses, shutter speeds, filters, and lighting designs are but a few of the things that get tested during this process.

Make sure you have enough time in the last week of prep for a variety of camera tests so you can solve any technical and creative issues early on with the DOP. It gets very expensive after everyone sees the dailies to realize that something is not working and you need to reshoot the scene.

23. Pre-Shoots

A pre-shoot is exactly what it sounds like — a scene you shoot a few days before principal photography with a minimal crew. These scenes can be anything from a newscaster sitting at a news desk in a real TV station to reporters standing against a green screen to generic B-roll of traffic in the street or an actor walking by himself on a beach.

4

DIRECTING THE
SHOOTING SCHEDULE

Japanese director Akira Kurosawa described a film director
as being a front-line commanding officer. "Unless you know
every aspect and phase of the film-production process, you
can't be a movie director. A movie director is like a front-line
commanding officer. He needs a thorough knowledge of every
branch of the service, and if he doesn't command each division,
he cannot command the whole. —STEVEN PRINCE*

THE DIRECTOR'S TOP 3 CREATIVE PRODUCTION TEAM

The director of photography, production designer, and 1st assistant director are
the director's "Top 3 Creative Production Team" — but remember the industry
politics. Television is a producer's medium; feature films are a director's medium!

On a feature film, these 3 people work "*FOR* the director *WITH* the producers," but in television they work "*WITH* the director *FOR* the producers." Big
difference!

The Director/1st Assistant Director Relationship
Directors are not only responsible for interpreting the script visually and getting
performances from actors, they are also responsible for finishing the show on time
and within budget. In other words, you have to also be "financially responsible," or
you may end up having a very short career!

Not only do you need to know how to "shoot the script," you also need to
know how to "*shoot the schedule.*" The two people that share that responsibility
with you are the DOP and the 1st AD.

The Warrior's Camera: The Cinema of Akira Kurosawa (Princeton University Press, 1991)

Your working relationship with the 1st AD is going to be one of the most important partnerships you will have in this business. The 1st AD is responsible for organizing the director's time during prep and running the film set.

Again, keep in mind the "industry politics" of the situation: Are you directing a movie or a TV series? Directors interview and hire the 1st assistant director on a feature film while the production manager (or producer) hires the 1st assistant director on a TV series.

> The very nature of the 1st AD's job always has them "serving two masters": the *creative* (director, DOP, actors) and the *budget* (producers, production manager, accountants). As a matter of fact, on some TV series, the 1st assistant director could be called a "1st assistant producer" based on how much influence they have with the producers over the director.

You will have several meetings with the 1st assistant director during preproduction. Here's what you want to achieve during those meetings:

- **Go over the script** scene by scene to let the 1st AD know how you plan to shoot each one. Give them a list of the special equipment you need (crane, Steadicam, circle track, special lenses, insert car, etc.).
- A director's **shot list** can be used as a guide to help the 1st AD better organize and create the shooting schedule. With a good shot list, the 1st AD can use the number of camera setups the director wants per scene to help them "time" each shooting day (rather than just using the page count). Storyboards are also a good way to decide on scene and shooting times.
- Review the **one-liner** to discuss the scene order each day and how much time the 1st AD thinks it will take to shoot each scene.
- The **shooting times** are the periods the 1st AD figures it will take to shoot each scene. They have to decide how long each scene will take to shoot, what time they want to begin a scene, and what time they want to finish the scene. This gives the director and crew a guide of where they need to be at any given moment during the shooting day.
- Directors are not usually responsible for deciding the **scene shooting order**. This is essentially the DOP and 1st AD's job since the time

it takes to complete a scene is based mostly on the specific technical logistics of the scene, how long the lighting will take, and how many camera setups one has. As you discuss the shooting order with the DOP and 1st AD, always remember this "mantra": *Minimize the number of moves and camera setups!*

CREATING A SHOOTING SCRIPT FROM THE STORY SCRIPT

When a script is first written, it has no scene numbers and is unofficially called a "story script." These scripts usually have more "written exposition" to help the story flow evenly from one scene to the next, which helps the readers — who are usually producers, executives, actors, bankers, and private investors — better understand the story narrative.

Once a film goes into production, a "shooting script" (the story as seen by the camera) is created by the 1st AD in consultation with the director. This involves numbering the script, splitting up scenes so they make more sense logistically, and creating better scene descriptions based on the actual locations you will be filming.

For example: Take a scene that involves a character getting out of a car outside of a building, walking into the front lobby of that building, entering the elevator, and then appearing in the penthouse suite.

In the story script, this scene could easily be described and numbered as one scene. But since it's highly unlikely you will physically be able to follow this character from the exterior to the top floor in one shot, you could break the scene into: (Sc. 1) the exterior; (Sc. 2) entering the front lobby and then the elevator; (Sc. 3) in the elevator; (Sc. 4) entering the penthouse suite.

FIVE TYPES OF SCENES IN A SHOOTING SCRIPT

Here are five "types of scenes" to consider when breaking down any script. You should approach the filming of each of these "types" of scenes differently; they all contain unique elements affecting how you shoot a scene and the time it will take to do so.

Dialogue Scenes (Talking, talking, and more talking!)

These scenes should take less time to shoot than action scenes.

Action and Practical Special-Effect Scenes

These scenes include stunts and practical on-set special effects, and they usually take longer to shoot than dialogue scenes.

Visual FX Scenes

These scenes include all types of visual-effects shots: green screen, plate shots, crowd duplication, etc. They may take longer to shoot than dialogue scenes.

Key Scenes

These could be dialogue scenes or action scenes that establish the mood of a story and may require more time to shoot than "regular scenes" (i.e., any scenes that introduce characters or contain major story points).

Act-Break Scenes

These scenes are written specifically for episodic television series (or webseries) and are important because they are used to keep the audience "hooked" into coming back after the commercial. (Soap operas are a good example of this kind of hook into a commercial break.)

PREPPING YOUR SHOT LIST —
SCENE ORDER TO SHOOTING ORDER

Script Order Shot List

During your early prep (when you are also location scouting), you begin to create your first shot list in *scene (story) order*. Once you get the preliminary one-liner from the 1st AD, you cut-and-paste your scene order shot list into the *shooting order*. This lets you know how many shots (setups) you have to shoot per day.

Shooting Order Shot List

After I get the preliminary one-liner from the 1st AD, I write the number of shots per scene on the one-liner for each shooting day. These setup numbers tell me how many shots per day I have to shoot, and if I have too many (or too few) shots per day.

I then go over the schedule with the 1st AD and DOP to see if we can move scenes around to accommodate the number of shots. It may be that I have to reduce my shots.

Location Shot Listing with DOP and 1st AD

After you have completed your scene order shot list and your preliminary shooting order shot list, visit as many "locked" locations as you can with the DOP and 1st AD.

At each location, review every scene carefully to make sure your shot lists are based on the real location and you're aware how many scenes are scheduled to be shot that day. You will also need to factor in other logistics such as day/night transitions, lighting concerns, and location wrap times.

You now need to "do the math" and figure out realistically the number of shots/per scene/per shooting day using suggestions from the DOP and 1st AD.

Tip: An "average" 2-page dialogue scene with 2 characters can contain anywhere from 3–7 shots.

1. Wide Shot Master
2. 2 Shot
3. OS Person A
4. CU Person A
5. OS Person B
6. CU Person B
7. Insert

> Determining how long it could take to shoot all the scenes scheduled on a shooting day is not always based on how many pages you have to shoot that day. It usually depends on how many *camera set-ups* you have to shoot per day. So a 4-page dialogue scene should be easier and faster to shoot than a 2-page action scene.

HOW TO DETERMINE "AVERAGE" SCENE-SHOOTING TIMES

To figure out how long it could take to shoot a particular scene (based on number of shooting days, shooting hours per day, and camera setups per day) here's a simple 6-step "formula" you can use a guide.

Note: This "formula" is based on your final one-liner and how many camera setups you have per scene. These numbers are also based on the use of one camera or two cameras. (For the following example, I am using *one camera*.)

1. Determine the "average" pages per shooting day based on script length and number of budgeted shooting days.
    example: 100-page script and a 25-day shoot = *4 pages/day.*

2. Determine the "average" shooting hours of scenes per day based on the number of budgeted shooting hours per day and the number of scheduled scenes per day.
    example: 12-hour shooting day plus 1-hour lunch. 3 scenes are scheduled on Day 1. So 12 shooting hours divided by 3 scenes = *4 hours per scene.*

3. Divide each scene by the average pages per day.
    example: 3 scenes scheduled on Day 1 for a total of 4 ⅛ pages. Based on an average of 4 hours shooting per scene, this is the *prorated* shooting time per scene in a 12-hour day:
    Sc. 5 — 2 pages (= 6 hours)
    Sc. 9 — 1 page (= 2 hours)
    Sc. 17 — 1 ⅛ pages (= 4 hours)

4. Divide scenes into action and dialogue scenes per day.
    example: 3 scenes scheduled on Day 1. Average shooting time per action or dialogue scene in a 12-hour day:
    Sc. 5 (Dialogue) — 2 pages (= 5 hours)
    Sc. 9 (Action) — 1 page (= 4 hours)
    Sc. 17 (Dialogue) — 1 ⅛ pages (= 3 hours)

5. Add your camera setups per scene.

   example: Total of 20 camera setups for day:

   Sc. 5 (Dialogue) — 2 pages (6 shots in 5 hours)

   Sc. 9 (Action) — 1 page (10 shots in 4 hours)

   Sc. 17 (Dialogue) — 1 ⅛ pages (4 shots in 3 hours)

6. *Revise* your per-scene shooting hours and/or shots based on per-scene camera setups.

   example: A new total of 18 camera setups for day:

   Sc. 5 (Dialogue) — 2 pages (6 shots in 4 hours)

   Sc. 9 (Action) — 1 page (8 shots in 5 hours)

   Sc. 17 (Dialogue) — 1 ⅛ pages (4 shots in 3 hours)

5

UNDERSTANDING HUMAN BEHAVIOR

No art passes our conscience in the way film does,
and goes directly to our feelings, deep down into the
dark rooms of our souls. —INGMAR BERGMAN

The main purpose of this chapter is to give you an overview of some basic human behaviors that *motivate* us in our daily lives, and how you can apply these "universal" behaviors to your own stories and films.

OBSERVING HUMAN BEHAVIOR

People are extremely complex, so figuring out the different ways our minds work is never an easy task. Everything we do is influenced by a variety of experiences: our native culture, our current circumstances and situation, and our genetic makeup and physical appearance.

Filmmakers are artists. Like all good artists, we have a driving internal need to tell our version of the human condition. But to effectively create our own "compelling stories with believable characters," we need to first know the different factors affecting the human mind. We can then better understand how (and why) people act and talk.

We must make it a priority to find out what makes us "tick" and discover what motivates us to do certain things. We must understand the importance of self-esteem and body language. We must understand why different cultures and environments affect us and cause us to act in certain ways.

If we really want to understand people, we need to constantly *observe* how people make sense of the world they live in. The good thing about human behavior is that it is observable, and as storytellers we must carefully watch the way people react to different situations and circumstances in order to know "why and how" their behavior changes.

UNDERSTANDING OURSELVES/UNDERSTANDING OTHERS

Human behavior (how we act) refers to our actions based on different personal factors such as our attitudes, character traits, and social beliefs. And because our physiological needs can influence our perceptions of others, the way we make sense of the world has a direct influence on our interactions.

Each of us live different lives (with distinct experiences) and our ideas and attitudes can be similar, or different, from one person to the next. And since we are all affected by our combined life experiences, we can be influenced by a great many factors.

For example: Our behavior can be greatly influenced by the rules and social beliefs that govern our individual groups and societies. Our behavior can be affected by each individual's faith (religion or philosophy).

Our behavior can be impacted by our individual genetics that vary from person to person, and it can also be influenced by our physical state. Are we physically, emotionally, and mentally healthy? Or are we stressed out and physically or mentally unhealthy?

There is never one reason why a person does something. People do things for lots of different reasons, some of which are completely unconscious, so looking for just one reason for someone's actions could lead to serious misunderstandings.

An important factor in how we see ourselves is our interpretation of how other people see us. Other people's reactions and ideas matter to us, and they greatly influence how we act in life because we tend to judge what we are like by the ways other people think of us and how they respond to us.

WHAT MAKES US DIFFERENT?

Our Society and Culture

Social beliefs are powerful, shared ideologies which can direct the actions of whole societies. These "group" beliefs have a strong influence on how we interpret certain events, how we explain what is going on to ourselves, and how we act. So to understand a person, you must also understand their society and culture. So much of what we learn as we grow up is about acting in the ways "our society" expects.

For example, Western cultures see a person as a separate individual who can choose to belong to any social group, but African cultures see a person as being a member of a community whose lifestyle choices affect the rest of the community.

Different cultures can also make biased assumptions about individuals and what it is to be a human being. People with different cultural and social beliefs often end up talking past one another, which can result in them not understanding each other — or worse!

The Time Period In Which We Live

Human behavior can vary from one period of history to another, and from one environment to another as society changes. For example, longevity, living standards, public health, and education 500 years ago were much different than they are today.

We are also partly influenced by our genes and our evolutionary history. What we learn (and how we learn) is different in each generation and each culture.

Where We Live and Work

Where we live, work, and play shapes us throughout our lives. We act, and react, completely differently in some environments than we do in others because we tend to adjust our behavior to different situations.

Since our behavior is also based on our society's (and culture's) image of how we are supposed to act and survive in a particular environment, we must adapt our behavior to those surroundings in which only certain kinds of actions are allowed. So if we are in a church or in a prison, how we act is based on that particular environment.

Different environments also affect us by encouraging us to do things we might not normally do, like going to a sports game where we dress up, yell, and do crazy things we would never think of doing at home or at work.

Our Personal Space

We tend to use distance to tell us about our relationship with other people. Everyone is surrounded by a little "bubble of personal space." We only allow people inside this space if we know them well enough, and different cultures have contrasting ideas of how big that bubble is. When we meet people, we generally respond differently to strangers than to people we are familiar with, so when talking to a stranger we tend to stand farther away from them than we would with a friend.

Even when people are very close to each other, the amount of contact they have depends on the culture they live in or grew up in. Example: People usually stand closer to each other in Middle Eastern cultures and farther apart in North American cultures.

Body Language (Nonverbal Communication)

Most people tend to believe nonverbal communication (*subtext*) more than the words (*text*) that are actually said. We usually pay more attention to a person's body language and tone of voice than we do to their actual words.

Facial expressions, posture, gestures and tone of voice are all important indicators of our attitudes and feelings, and we need to be able to understand these feelings so we have some idea of how we should respond to them.

People often convey a lot of extra information by the words they choose and how they say them. It helps to listen to the pattern of words people use to find out what they are really saying — or not saying! (i.e., politician "bafflegab")

Eye contact is one of the most powerful communication signals of all. When we look directly into someone's eyes, they have our undivided attention. And if we don't want contact or we don't want to disturb people, we tend to look away from them.

Self-Esteem (Self-Worth)

Each of us have our own idea about what we are like, how we think, and what we are good or bad at doing. Healthy self-esteem is our ability to accept who we are by recognizing our strengths and weaknesses and our value as a person.

It's a basic human need to look for sources of positive self-esteem by belonging to social groups that influence our sense of identity. Two psychological needs that have to be satisfied in order to have good self-esteem are the need for positive consideration from other people (love, affection, trust) and the need for exploring and developing our own abilities (talents, ideas, interests).

Our level of self-esteem also depends on the type of personal relationships we have, both in the past and in the present. Fortunately, most people have always had a reasonably high level of self-esteem, but problems can arise when our need for approval from others is in direct conflict with our own abilities.

People with low self-esteem usually have unrealistic conditions of worth (they see themselves as failures or as inferior to other people) and they tend to look for positive experiences to compensate for their negative thoughts and feelings, even if these feelings are only temporary.

Basic Human Needs

Human needs are an important part of our nature. Values, beliefs, and customs differ from country to country, but we all have similar needs, and these needs are powerful personal motivators.

According to Abraham Maslow's "Hierarchy of Needs,"* there are two major groups of human needs: "basic needs" and "higher needs."

Basic needs are *physiological*, such as food, water, shelter, and sleep; and *psychological*, such as affection, security, safety, and self-esteem. If these basic needs are not met, we will always try to make up the deficiency.

Higher needs are called *growth needs*. These include needs such as knowledge, justice, goodness, beauty, order, etc.

Every day people all over the world strive to meet their individual needs and goals, but if our basic needs are not met, they then become the main object of our daily goals. Our personal basic needs are the most urgent.

Higher needs will become a "motive of behavior" as long as the basic needs have been met. But unsatisfied basic needs must always be filled first, before a person can satisfy their higher or growth needs.

---

*Abraham Harold Maslow, *Motivation and Personality* (Harper & Row, 1954)

THE OBSERVATION BUSINESS

As artists and filmmakers, we need to prioritize *understanding human behavior* by observing people going about their daily lives. This reveals what actually motivates them to take action — **and we can then apply these real human traits to our fictional characters!**

Once you know what "really" motivates a person to take action, you will better understand your story, have a clearer idea how to block your scenes, and feel more confident guiding your actors to believable performances.

As writers and directors, it's our job to continuously dig deeper into this act of observation, so we must practice the art of observing human behavior every day. As storytellers, we are all in the "observation business."

> Airports are great places to study the "flip side of human behavior" because you can quickly observe two common human emotions by simply walking from the departures level to the arrivals level. At the departures level, you will see *sadness* (tears, abandonment, loneliness) and at the arrivals level you will see *happiness* (tears, completion, togetherness).

6

WHAT MAKES A
GOOD STORY?

Drama is real life with the dull bits cut out.
—ALFRED HITCHCOCK

The next four chapters are not about how to write a good screenplay. They are about how to make the best film from the script you have now by understanding the key elements that make up a good story.

As filmmaking technology gets better and more sophisticated, it has given young filmmakers all over the world an opportunity to tell their own stories about the human condition without having to worry about expensive equipment, large crews, or big budgets.

Even though filmmaking is not as expensive or complicated as it was several years ago, the technology you are using today will never guarantee you can make a great film.

While improved logistical tools and creative techniques allow filmmakers to tell more complex visual stories, *the art of good storytelling* will always remain the same. It's a basic fact that audiences everywhere still want to go to a movie and be rewarded for their time by watching *a compelling story with believable characters who make them feel something.*

Note: There are literally thousands of books and articles that discuss the screenwriting process in depth, so for the next four chapters I let my good friend and screenwriter Michael Bruce Adams contribute some of his experiences and thoughts on "What makes a good story?"

WHAT MAKES A GOOD STORY?

By Michael Bruce Adams

Good story ideas can come from anywhere: dreams, articles, images, something you hear in a restaurant. But in order to make a good story idea great, it must be developed.

To most audiences a good story is exciting, well paced, and complex. Complexity is the only one of these traits driven by story ideas; the others have to do with execution. Audiences sometimes wrongly believe that good stories are complex, when in fact the best stories have strong, simple goals with characters that may be complex. *They* are actually what we love in stories.

To find the strongest story goals and the right characters to go after those goals, explore your ideas through a series of questions:

What is your rough idea? What do you want to tell a story about?
You have a spark . . . now you need to find the essence of that idea. How you get there is your own process. Do you need to write a scene to discover its essence, or a short story, or have a coffee with a friend and talk it over?

What is the element within your idea that really moves you and excites you?
Is there a moment between two people that you can see clear as day in your mind's eye? Is there a collage of sound that you can hear . . . a taste . . . a smell . . . an instant that brings you to laughter or tears?

What different possibilities can you think of to tell this story?
If your idea began with an image or event, where within the screen story do you feel that event takes place? What comes before the event? What results occur directly after the event? If your idea is an issue, how do you see a character's journey illuminating that issue?

What are some of the challenges involved in this story idea?
Do you risk alienating some of your audience because of how your characters illuminate a point of view or belief? Is that okay? Are there logistical challenges?

What is the designing principle of this story?
The worst type of scenario we can create for a lead character would be based on

their wound or internal struggle. We force our heroes to face their fears, own up to a past sin, leap into the unknown. What is the journey initiated by this challenge?

Who is the best character to live out this idea?

Which character's internal journey is intensified by the physical journey to the best effect? In other words, over the course of solving the central problem of the story, which character will be transformed the most by the journey?

What is the story world that our hero's journey moves through?

What are the physical and emotional rules of existence for our hero? Do they have superpowers? Do they have crippling fears? How does their behavior reflect the rules of their life? How does the setting and the culture of the story world create barriers for the hero?

What is the conflict? Who is the hero fighting, and what are they fighting for?

There are usually several conflicts in great stories. We want to identify the main conflict first, then secondary ones. The best stories have a series of conflicts with opponents who complement each other so that the tension builds from one to the next.

What is the basic sequence of events, the action path that the hero must take?

From our work on the prior questions, we know that the plot of a story is not simple to create. Because we want an organic, truthfully motivated series of events, we strike a note of caution before plotting them out. Allow yourself to revise the plot as you go through the last series of questions.

What is the wound that the hero must heal in order to be successful?

We're connecting the overarching motivation to the ultimate success of our hero. The backstory event that created our lead's character flaw is the wound that must be healed. We see evidence that the wound has been healed when the hero overcomes their flaw and succeeds in their goal . . . or better still, turns their flaw into an advantage that allows them to become successful.

What is the transformation your hero experiences?

Near the end of your story, the lead character will experience a revelation about themselves and how the world has changed around them as the result of their journey. The revelation should be directly associated with the healing of the wound.

What is the moral challenge or decision your hero faces at the beginning of the story — and then at the end of the story?
Because the hero's transformation is often internal, the audience needs visual evidence of what has occurred. A moral decision or challenge will show the audience, through the hero's choice, how he or she has changed. An effective transformation shows our hero making the exact opposite choice at the end of the journey than they would have at the beginning.

Once we put our story idea through this development process, we should have a very deep understanding of who our lead character is and a strong sense of their motivations and goals. Conflicts and action path give us a sense of a possible plotline. The hero's transformation and revelation give us theme, emotional foundation, and story direction.

If any of your answers to these questions seem ambiguous or vague, keep working. Great stories start with good bones . . . at this stage of the process we want answers with simplicity, clarity, and concise language.

STORY AND PLOT

By Michael Bruce Adams
Depending on who is doing the story analyzing (writer, director, film critic), you can have varied perceptions of what story is and what plot is.

From a writer's perspective, **story** is every element that goes into building the narrative opus that will inspire the next Golden Globe: story structure, characters, subtext, dialogue, plot, and many other components.

Plot, in its simplest expression, is the story events in sequence that your characters (the hero, and his or her allies and opponents) journey through.

There is some confusion about the importance of plot in writing. Due to a glut of feature films that were heavy on plot and low on character (which translates to low on substance), filmgoers began craving anti-plot films. I don't even know what the heck that means.

Plot is vital to story. *John Truby in his book *The Anatomy of Story* tells us that plot and character are two sides of the same story coin. I agree. Plot should be

---

*John Truby, *The Anatomy of Story: 22 Steps to Becoming a Master Storyteller* (Faber & Faber, 2007)

treated with the same respect and care in the story-structure process as character, subtext, motivation, etc.

When most writers begin setting up a story, they think of plot first. They try to get down a cool sequence of events that their characters can sink their teeth into. Unfortunately, that means they have to pigeonhole their characters, regardless of the transformational story arcs and motivations, into that "cool sequence of events." Or worse, reverse-engineer character arcs based on that cool sequence of events. (Shudder!)

The key to understanding plot and building great plots is to *view plot as the result of your characters' motivations, decisions, and actions.*

Motivate your hero into making their first decision. The action they take from that decision, and their reaction to the result, will naturally motivate their next decision and action. If you work to find the broadest spectrum of truthfully motivated possibilities for your hero's decisions, actions, and reactions, you will never run out of ideas or end up in a clichéd situation. Your plot "organically" moves forward based on realistic motivation.

DRAMA AND CONFLICT

> Without conflict there is no action; without action there is no character; without character there is no story. And without story there is no screenplay. —SYD FIELD, *Screenplay: The Foundations of Screenwriting* (Dell Publishing, 1979)

Conflict goes to the very heart and essence of storytelling — without conflict, there is no drama! Good drama shows characters in confrontation with each other because they have opposite objectives. And when you put characters in conflict, the audience experiences this conflict and is drawn to the story.

No Conflict
A man comes home from work.
Husband — "How was your day, dear?"
Wife — "I had a great day. And how was your day, dear?"
Husband — "My day was great."

Little Conflict

A man comes home from work.

Husband — "How was your day, dear?"

Wife — "I had a great day. And how was your day, dear?"

Husband — "I just got fired!"

More Conflict

A man comes home from work.

Husband — "How was your day, dear?"

Wife — "I saw the doctor today, and we're going to have twins!"

Husband — "Oh my God! I just got fired!"

Eight Sources of Conflict

1. Man Against Man
   Example: *Hell in the Pacific* — Lee Marvin
2. Man Against Himself
   Example: *A Beautiful Mind* — Russell Crowe
3. Man Against Nature
   Example: *Twister* — Bill Paxton
4. Man Against Society
   Example: *Philadelphia* — Tom Hanks
5. Man Against Supernatural
   Example: *Ghostbusters* — Bill Murray
6. Man Against Machine/Technology
   Example: *The Terminator* — Arnold Schwarzenegger
7. Man Against Destiny/Fate
   Example: *Excalibur* — Nigel Terry
8. Man Against God/Principle
   Example: *The Mission* — Robert De Niro

TEXT, SUBTEXT, AND CONTEXT

By Michael Bruce Adams

Text is the script, what is written on the page. Text implies subtext and delivers context.

Subtext means the underlying core themes and emotional foundations of a story. Subtext can be implied in the text through the suggestion of technical and artistic choices, but it is never overtly expressed. Elements of context can be used to express subtext, but likewise never overtly.

Context is the "who," "what," "where," "when," and "how" parameters of a story. Context elements can be found in the text.

From a writer's perspective, subtext, or more specifically how we communicate subtext, is one of the most gratifying screenwriting processes, but very few people ever really perceive or comprehend what we've done when we do it well.

We use shorter sentences and tighter dialogue to suggest faster edits and raise the heart rate of the reader.

We describe patterns and shapes that speak of a historical design period to inspire nostalgia.

We describe color, light, and textures to imply a soft, welcoming atmosphere or a hard, cold tone.

Our characters gladly take out the garbage when we want to talk about devoted love.

If subtext is expressed well by a filmmaker through every department from props to sound, the result is that rare thing: a story that can be perfectly understood and engaging without dialogue.

And why, you ask, as a writer would I advocate such a thing?

When you don't NEED dialogue, you are free to truly create transcendent spoken elements: simple conversations that illuminate deep emotion, wordplay between characters, and when you need it . . . silence.

So how do we express subtext in our filmmaking?

One way to think about subtext is in relation to time:

Entire story: Overall themes, super-objectives, internal and external goals, primary motivations . . . these are story elements that work within the context of the entire story. Overall, subtextual decisions work throughout the entire film to support these story elements; they can be used early in the story to prime the audience to remember certain themes and ideas.

Scene sequences: Each sequence is a mini-story with its own context that drives the lead character in a new direction. Each sequence has a significant place within the story structure. Each sequence has its own objectives and motivational nuances. All this specific information within the context of the scene sequence can be supported by subtext.

The subtext elements can support the overall themes to remind the audience that this sequence is part of an entire story, or they can support the specific themes and objectives of only the scene sequence . . . or they can do both.

Moments in time: Each frame of our film exists as a moment in time that is informed by everything that has come before, and could be foreshadowed with all that will come after. Each frame can be viewed like a painting that can speak to the viewer on many levels.

Subtext helps to decode the vast number of motivations that are working on our characters at any given point in time. Subtext will also support the scene sequence that is the larger context for each image, and of course, the overall story themes.

Backstory: One of the most difficult things a filmmaker must do is eliminate the need to spend valuable screen-story time on backstory exposition. Any screen time used in explaining backstory is time we have to take away from telling our main story.

The events in our characters' lives prior to the story are incredibly important in developing character and motivation, but not part of the context of our story. If they are relevant to our story, however, they can and should be considered as subtext.

Subtext, in regards to backstory, means providing clues to the key events in our characters' pasts that have relevance and importance to the story we are telling. There is no need for anything else.

Unless the story demands a nonlinear structure, flashbacks, voiceover, and excessive exposition can all be eliminated with thoughtful use of subtext.

Foreshadowing: These are subtext elements that give clues about events that will happen in the future of your story, or after the context of your story. Foreshadowing works best if used in a very restrained and subtle way. The last thing that we want to do as filmmakers is give away too much of our story.

Remember that applying subtext in your writing and filmmaking is a series of choices . . . you are deciding which clues or revelations you will provide to your audience, and which things you will hold back.

THEMES AND UNIVERSAL THEMES

By Michael Bruce Adams

In the same way that the collective consciousness of a society can recognize both ancient and modern symbology, certain themes can be understood through many generations and cross-culturally. We call these themes *universal*.

To really understand themes though we must examine the core of what they are in art . . . the artist's moral point of view. The artist may have a popular point of view (their moral interpretation of an idea could be widely agreed upon in broad strokes), but each person's point of view is as unique as a fingerprint.

When we turn our lenses to our characters' moral actions, we do so with judgment as to whether their actions are right or wrong, whether they have integrity or are compromised. When those actions and judgments are about vital life experiences such as how we view death, there is an expectation that these beliefs are common among humanity. But it is through the subtle and sometimes not-so-subtle contrasts of beliefs that a theme may be more profoundly explored. Simply put, when our characters agree with each other our stories are boring, but when they argue about the core themes in our stories, our films become challenging and illuminating.

It is sometimes impossible for people of different cultures to relate to culturally specific themes. A community that practices respect for the dead by never touching the cadaver cannot comprehend a corpse-dismemberment ritual practiced elsewhere.

Even with the challenges of finding truly universal themes, stories intended for international audiences must attempt to include thematic elements that speak universally. Successful universal elements typically reference ancient codes passed down from generation to generation based on life experiences rather than beliefs.

For example, how we enter life (bathed in birth blood) and exit life (bleeding death blood) has created a core human reaction to the color red. Red can have myriad meanings in cultural, national, and community beliefs, ranging from love to danger to good fortune, but all humanity recognizes red as being associated with blood, life, and death.

> Some *common universal themes* are abandonment, coming of age, death & dying, family & relationships, fear & courage, loss of innocence, growing up, good vs. evil, morals & values, loneliness, patriotism, taking a stand.

7

UNDERSTANDING
STORY STRUCTURE

*The screenplay is the same as it has always been; a screenplay is
a story told with pictures, in dialogue and description, and placed
within the context of dramatic structure. That's what it is; that is
its nature. It is the art of visual storytelling.* —SYD FIELD*

WHAT IS STORY STRUCTURE?

By Michael Bruce Adams

From a director's perspective, trying to direct a story without understanding story
structure is like trying to drive a car without a steering wheel . . . you might be okay
for the first few seconds, but there is absolutely no hope that things will end well.

As critical as story structure is to storytelling, coming up with a simple definition of "story structure" is not an easy task. We might try . . .

*Story structure is a choreographed sequence of truthfully motivated decisions,
actions, reactions, and revelations that a central character executes and experiences
in pursuit of a compelling and tangible goal.*

or . . .

*Story structure is the dramatic sequence formed when a transformational
lead-character arc is intimately combined with a compelling and truthfully motivated plot.*

Both these statements may be accurate, but how each writer and director
approaches story structure (and chooses their techniques, priorities, and emotional inspiration) yields blueprints that are as unique as the stories those writers
and directors create.

---

*Screenplay: The Foundations of Screenwriting (Dell Publishing, 1979)

Storytelling at its finest is a precise engineering of technique and design. The very finest story structure persuades an audience to feel that the story is organic and authentic while utilizing a process that is as calculated and intentional as art can be.

So how do we apply such a vast yet exacting concept to our work? Let's look at what makes up good story structure . . . through the individual elements, we might see the whole.

Let's start from the beginning.

Story structure has been refined and become more sophisticated since the time of Aristotle, Gilgamesh before him, and the fine artists who drew the Paleolithic cave paintings in Lascaux, France 30,000 years before all of us. Yet the basics of story structure have not changed; they are embedded in the human experience.

We are problem-solving beings. Our art and our stories are reflective of the great problems of our times.

In Lascaux 30,000 years ago, the problem was: *How do we eat in the winter when all the roots and berries are gone?* From that we have what is quite possibly the world's first symbolized narrative: hunters, in order to feed a starving community, sharpen sticks and brave the winter cold to kill and bring back a bison. And luckily for us they had the skills to tell their story.

This new way of providing meant the ancient people of Lascaux did not have to migrate south for the winter months, or were at least able to limit their migration. Empowered, they were inspired to write down their story on the cave walls near their community. The hunters were depicted as small figures compared to the life-giving beasts that dominate the paintings. The bison brings life, like the sun that dominates art after the hunter-gatherer period and the man-gods that dominate art and story after that.

So we're problem solvers. We live small stories a thousand times a day. Every problem we face is a story being told.

Hungry? Got to make a plan to get food, got to sharpen sticks, got to go out and kill food, got to bring it back . . . and of course got to live to tell the tale.

We don't have to use a problem-solving structure; we can tell a story thousands of different ways. The dilemma is that we as human beings understand story best when it's *within a problem-solving structure*, and the further we move away from that structure, the less engaging our story will be.

Hungry? Yeah, but it's too cold outside . . . maybe if we wait long enough, a squirrel will come by.

Not very compelling, is it?

So we're trying to solve a problem, or meet a challenge, or achieve a goal. By the nature of those things . . . solve a problem, meet a challenge, achieve a goal . . . it is implied that we are lacking something or we would have already resolved this issue. We have a weakness. So before we can solve the problem, we have to learn something or train ourselves to meet this challenge.

Ladies and gentlemen, welcome to Act Two.

But hold on . . . before we get to the stick-sharpening/hunter-training montage, let's back up. Why exactly do we want to leave this warm cave? What is our motivation . . . the thing that gets us out of the cave and drives us forward?

Our hero may have a very strong desire to go and kill a bison, but as the builders of this story we need to know all the forces at work pushing our hero onward . . . and holding him or her back.

So let's say our hero wants to bring a bison back to the tribe, but he or she wants to do it in a very specific way: they want to hunt and kill a bison with a spear.

We want to devise a *weakness* for our hero that fits with achieving his or her goal; in this case, we could make our hero hopeless at spear-hunting.

From there we can reverse-engineer a reason for his spear ineptitude, something like: years ago, during another time of starvation, our hero was responsible for his brother's death in a hunting accident after their father forbade them to use spears.

From this we get a complex set of motivations: a *wound* (his guilt over the hunting accident) our hero has to struggle with and eventually heal if he wants to succeed, and a *deep subconscious need* (the need to prove to his father that he can hunt and provide for the tribe responsibly) that will have to be fulfilled in order for his effort to have meaning.

The great thing about this *backstory* information is that your audience doesn't need to know any of the details. You can use it for character and story structure development, and then use it as fuel for adding layers of subtextual elements in your storytelling.

With his painful history, an embarrassing weakness, and a driving need, our hero has very real and compelling emotional fuel to propel his journey. But more important to our visual story, we are creating an environment for our hero to experience a deep transformation if he or she succeeds.

All these motivational forces are the foundation of our *hero's transformational arc.*

From this foundation, our hero is going to make a series of decisions, and take action on those decisions with a plan to achieve his goal. The outcome of each decision will twist our hero into a new direction, but always move toward achieving the goal.

We want those decisions to be logical and realistic for someone like our hero, and at the same time be surprising and unexpected. We want each event to reveal a new aspect about our hero, about his weaknesses and vulnerabilities or his strengths . . . or, even better, about both. We want the physical and emotional stakes to become more intense as our hero progresses. We want the physical and emotional battles our hero wages to rise to a crescendo and be resolved in a spectacular fashion. We want our hero's final revelation to reflect his transformation from the beginning of the story in a profound way. This sequence of events based on our hero's decisions and actions can be called our *hero's plotline.*

So if character + plot = story structure, then story = story structure + everything else.

So . . . after all this, have we managed to come to a definitive explanation of story structure? Well, sort of . . .

Story structure is a choreographed sequence of truthfully motivated decisions, actions, reactions, and revelations that a central character executes and experiences in pursuit of a compelling and tangible goal.

My feeling is that for *directors* this definition may have more relevance in terms of getting the best performances from their actors.

and . . .

Story structure is the dramatic sequence formed when a transformational lead character arc is intimately combined with a compelling and truthfully motivated plot.

And this definition might be more relevant to *writers* who are working to develop great story ideas.

So two definitions. I know . . . sue me, I'm a writer.

JOSEPH CAMPBELL AND THE HERO'S JOURNEY

Joseph Campbell (1904–1987) was an American mythologist and writer best known for his work in the fields of religion and mythology.

After years of extensive research, Campbell discovered that various myths and stories from cultures around the world (and from different time periods) all seemed to share a universal "storytelling" pattern with similar stages that he called the "monomyth" or the *hero's journey*.

> A hero ventures forth from the world of common day into a region of supernatural wonder: fabulous forces are there encountered and a decisive victory is won: the hero comes back from this mysterious adventure with the power to bestow boons on his fellow man. —JOSEPH CAMPBELL, *The Hero with a Thousand Faces* (Princeton University Press, 1949)

Campbell's "hero's journey" has now become the basic model used in most modern storytelling (films, novels, plays, etc.) because it divides a fictional story into a simple *3-act structure*: The Setup (Act One); the Confrontation (Act Two); and the Resolution (Act Three).

Here is a simplified outline of Campbell's 3-act structure. (Also from the book by Christopher Vogler, *The Writer's Journey: Mythic Structure for Writers* (Michael Wiese Productions, 2007).)

SEPARATION (Act One: The Setup)
1. The Mundane World
The hero is introduced in ordinary surroundings

2. The Call to Adventure
Something new enters his life — a catalyst

3. Refusal of the Call
The reluctant hero — he has to be personally motivated

4. The Protective Figure
A protecting power (mentor) who helps the hero

5. Supernatural Aid
An amulet (charm) given by the protective figure

6. The Threshold Guardian
The first demon the hero encounters before he can cross

7. The Belly of the Whale
The hero crosses the threshold into the unknown

INITIATION (Act Two: The Confrontation)
1. The Road of Trials
Tests and obstacles the hero must face to attain his goal

2. The Helpers/Guardians
Symbolic figures that give advice and amulets

3. Meeting With the Goddess/the Temptress (Love/Truth)
The darkness of the heart is overcome to win the boon

4. Atonement With the Father
The hero opens his Soul (Ego) to seek Source (Truth)

5. The Black Moment
The hero hits bottom — a death experience (Rebirth)

6. Highest Development/Apotheosis
Hero seizes the sword and takes the treasure

7. The Ultimate Boon
The symbol of life energy — spiritual growth

RETURN (Act Three: The Resolution)
1. Refusal of Return
Some heroes refuse their responsibility and never return

2. The Magic Flight — Resented
The hero is chased back by the demons

3. The Magic Flight — Blessed
The hero is supported on his return by guardians

4. Rescue from Without
The "world" may have to come and get the hero

5. Crossing the Return Threshold
Hero must face one final ordeal — survive the crossing

6. Transformation
The hero is reborn and is reintegrated into his society

7. Master of Two Worlds/Blessed With Vision
The hero has the freedom to pass between two worlds

> When George Lucas wrote *Star Wars*, he very carefully followed
> Campbell's 3-act story structure, which is one reason it was such a
> popular story with audiences around the world.

THE CLASSIC THREE-ACT STRUCTURE

Whenever I begin my script analysis process as a director, I use the three-act story structure model because it's the simplest and most common film narrative story structure there is.

This is because no matter what your story is about, or your visual style in shooting the film, or how it will eventually be edited together, every good story that has ever been told has a *beginning*, a *middle*, and an *end*!

Here's the simple *3-act story structure breakdown* I use to answer my first questions about any script I am directing.

By answering these 15 basic questions first, I get a quick overview of what the story is about; who the main character is; who or what the antagonist is; what problem has to be solved; what the "hero's journey" is; how the problem is solved at the end of the story; and what eventually happens to all the characters.

Act One (Setup/Separation)

Act One is where the main characters are introduced. We see the world they live in as well as their relationships with other characters. A problem is then introduced that the protagonist (main character/hero) has to deal with. This problem, and how the main character addresses it, drive the story forward.

Example: New boy in town meets girl — but her father doesn't like him.

- What is the situation? (Story/plot)
- What is the theme? (What the story is *really* about)
- Who is the protagonist? (Main character/hero)
- Who is the main antagonist? (Main opposition/bad guy)
- What is the inciting incident? (Life-changing event)

Act Two (Confrontation/Initiation)

In Act Two, the protagonist goes through major changes in his or her life in an effort to resolve the problem created in Act One (Inciting Incident), only to find they are getting into ever-worsening situations.

Example: Boy loses girl and fights against impossible odds to get her back.

- What is the main problem the protagonist has to solve? (Physical, psychological)
- What obstacles stand in the protagonist's way? (What characters, events, or inner weaknesses stops the protagonist from achieving their goal?)
- How does the protagonist overcome each obstacle? (Actions)
- What is the B-story? (Usually the love story)
- What is the "all is lost" moment? (The point where the protagonist almost dies physically or emotionally)

Act Three (Resolution/Return)

In Act Three, the main character tries one last time to solve the problem presented in Act One, and the main character comes to understand the meaning of the underlying theme (message) of the film. It's also where all the other story elements, subplots, and character relationships get resolved.

Example: Boy gets the girl and they live happily ever after . . . or not!

- How does the protagonist solve the main problem? (Actions)
- How does the story end? (Closed ending or open ending)
- What happens to the protagonist?
- What happens to the antagonist?
- What happens to the other characters?

SCRIPT AND SCENE ANALYSIS

Good scripts are complex with a rich subworld hinted at and not over-explained. Bad scripts are often over-explained and obvious. —JUDITH WESTON*

THE DIRECTOR AND THE STORY

There are many phases of the director's preproduction on any film — from location scouts and creative meetings to casting and shot listing — but the first, and most important part of your job, is to *understand the story.*

courtesy Mehtap Kizilirmak

Understanding the story requires a lot of work. You need to break down the script and analyze each individual scene to discover: what the story is (really) about; what the main theme is; what the story points are; who the main characters are; and what happens to them.

Your script breakdown will be a never-ending process. Every time you review your script, or have meetings with department heads about the script, you will discover different things about the story or the characters you did not know before.

And the script will also constantly

Directing Actors: Creating Memorable Performances for Film & Television (Michael Wiese Productions, 1996) change and evolve because of your creative notes, writer notes, actor notes, producer notes, studio/network notes, location availability problems, and scheduling conflicts. But as long as you know what the story is about and where it's is going, you will be able to adjust to all the changes.

Remember: a director is a storyteller, and to be a good storyteller you need to first understand every detail about the story you are telling. No matter what part of the production process you are in, whenever you make a logistical or creative decision, ask yourself, "*Does the decision I am making now serve the story?*"

THE STORY LOGLINE

By Michael Bruce Adams

As a director, knowing the logline, or premise, is the single most important tool to track your story from script to screen. Why are loglines so important?

Loglines are the crystalized expressions of a story idea. Loglines provide the essential elements at a glance to keep the creative process on track and moving forward. Loglines provide both the story touchstone for every aspect of production and the hero's main goals and conflicts.

What are the key elements of an effective logline?

1. A hero begins an *external journey* . . . (physical arc, problem to solve)
2. . . . and fights an *internal struggle* . . . (emotional arc, moral dilemma)
3. . . . while up against the *main conflict* with the *primary opponent* . . . (Who stands in the way of the hero achieving his or her goals? How do they do this?)
4. . . . in order to *achieve* the *tangible external goal* . . . (the hero will either solve the problem at the end of the journey or not)

The language we use for creating loglines is full of clichés and simple language; it is meant to be. Unfocused loglines lead to confusing, exposition-laden storytelling. We want to use the simplest, most impactful language to communicate our themes and ideas.

Here are some examples of movie loglines that work:

Whiplash logline: A driven conservatory student must overcome the abuse of an acclaimed bandleader in order to become the best jazz drummer in the world.

Moneyball logline: A jilted baseball general manager turns to an unpopular new approach, in spite of sabotage from his chief scout and manager, in order to give his team a winning chance.

Jaws logline: A cowardly policeman battles a greedy community and an obsessed hunter before going on a suicidal mission to save his community from a man-eating shark.

Gravity logline: A grieving astronaut is trapped in space after a catastrophic accident and must turn her grief into determination in order to return to Earth alive.

GENERAL STORY ANALYSIS

Your First Impressions of the Story

When you first get your script, read it through once so you can quickly discover what the story is about, where it takes place, who the characters are, and what happens to them. This quick reading is very important; it's when you form your *first impressions* of the story — plus it's probably the only time you will enjoy the script. From now on, it's all work!

As you read the script, make note of your emotional reaction to the story and what images the story stimulates in you. Your initial reactions represent what an audience could feel when they see the movie for the first time. What you feel when you read the script really counts; it is your *emotional* response to the story that will define your reactions as "truth."

What is your emotional reaction to the story? (What attracted you to the story when you first read it?)

What initial images and sounds does the story stimulate in you? (Visuals, colors, designs, locations, costumes, sounds, music, shots)

What is the story genre? (Comedy, drama, horror, mystery, fantasy, etc.)

What is the dramatic style of the story? (Fiction drama, nonfiction drama, docudrama)

Where are the locations of the story? (What country, city, language?)

In what time period does the story take place? (Do the action, dialogue, rhythm, and color of this period feel true?)

Then read the script again. This second reading begins the long process of understanding the events and characters of the story. You accomplish this by *asking a lot of questions*, which is the most important part of your script analysis; questions lead to research, which leads to answers.

Asking questions gives you a better understanding of the story situation, problem, or challenge; your answers to these questions will become progressively clearer after each reading of the script.

Story Themes

A *theme* is the central idea, message, or lesson within a story the author wants to convey to the viewer. A *universal theme* allows people from different cultures to emotionally connect to the story because it features common (universal), applicable life experiences.

What *do you feel* is the main theme or message of the story? (What is the writer trying to say about the human condition?)

Does this story (plot and theme) affect you personally? (What do you want to say? What are your personal points of view?)

What are the different ways (dramatic metaphors) the theme is being expressed in the story? (What specific lines of dialogue, characters, plot situations, visuals, symbols, colors, sounds, or music express the main theme?)

What does the story title mean to you? (Does the title "appear" somewhere in the story? Is the title part of the theme? Will a potential viewer go to this movie because of the title?)

Story Logic

Story logic questions help you find the overall strengths, weaknesses, and potential problems of the story. Remember, if something doesn't make sense in the script, it won't make sense when you shoot it and it won't make sense to the audience when they see the movie.

Do the events (plot) in the story logically add up? (Does the story structure make sense? Do the scene transitions flow smoothly together?)

What scenes do you like, and why? (Do these scenes reveal information and move the story forward?)

What happens next in every scene? (Did you anticipate the result, or was it a surprise?)

What scenes don't make sense, and why? (Are you confused about a character, line of dialogue, plot point, or action?)

Story Events

Story events are actions or dialogue that happen in the scene, and once they take place they become fact. (Example 1: The main story event in *Pearl Harbor* was the Japanese surprise attack. Example 2: The main story event in *Titanic* is the sinking of the ship after it hits an iceberg.)

Story Facts

Story facts are situations, actions, or events that *actually happen* in the story. They are not subject to interpretation because they are, in fact, FACT! Anytime there is more than one possible explanation for something in the script, it is not a fact.

DETAILED STORY ANALYSIS

Now that you have answered some general questions about the story, it's time to go into specific detail about the overall story.

What is the **plot**? (This is the A-story that carries the action.)

What is the **subplot**? (This is the B-story that usually carries the theme.)

What is the **inciting incident**? (This is the event in Act One that happens to the main character. This event, or incident, forces them to take some kind of action and sets the story in motion.)

What is the **spine** of the story? (The spine is basically the reason for the character's journey. It's what the character wants, and the spine of the main character usually runs parallel to the central theme of the script.)

In any film, a character should have only one spine for the whole story. To find a character's spine, look for his or her transforming event (in Act 1) and its end result (in Act 3).

What is the **main question** to be answered? (This is the main character's problem (situation) set up in Act 1 that has to be solved by the end of Act 3.)

What are all the **action points**? (These are all the dramatic events in the story that cause the main character to react in some way. These events could be physical or emotional.)

What (or who) is the main **source of conflict**? (This could be an event, situation, or person.)

Who is the **protagonist**? (This is the main character of the story; he or she takes the hero's journey.)

Who is the **antagonist**? (This is the main adversary the hero has to face throughout the story and who the hero must defeat by the end of the film.)

Is there a second **antagonist**? (This could be another person, a mental state, or a special environment. Examples: The schizophrenic brain of John Nash in *A Beautiful Mind*; the tornado in *Twister*; the planet Mars in *The Martian*; the sinking ship in *Titanic*.)

Who is the **most interesting character**? (This does not always have to be the main character.)

What is the **resolution/conclusion**? (How does the story end?)

What happens to all the characters? How is the theme resolved? (The ending should be worth the wait for an audience — it should be an event in itself.)

DETAILED SCENE-BY-SCENE ANALYSIS

Once you understand the story, who the characters are, and what happens to them, you now need to analyze each individual scene by digging deeper into the story and its structure. (*Note:* You will use many of the same story analysis points I mentioned above, but now they are specifically designed for each scene.)

Stage directions are the writer's ideas, suggestions, or concepts for the director and the actors that show or describe (a) backstory facts pertaining to a scene or a character (b) the behavior or inner life of a character (c) the staging or blocking the writer is thinking about and (d) various actor business.

You should always make note of the stage directions, but they don't always have to be treated as fact. Remember, it's your job as the director to "interpret the script visually" and stamp it with your unique vision.

> When experienced actors break down their scripts, they usually cross out any stage directions that tell them when their character should move or how the character should feel at that particular moment. Actors want to (and need to) discover those things for themselves!

What is the **main scene objective** (or intent) of the scene? Why is this scene in the story? What is the main reason for the scene? What is the scene used for dramatically? If you take this scene out of the script, will it affect the story? Does this scene move the story forward, or is it just used for character development?

Every scene in a film has at least *three* objectives: (1) to move the story forward (2) to reveal plot (3) to reveal character.

For the actor, a scene objective is something their character consciously wants to achieve, and this desire carries the character through a particular scene.

For the director, a scene could have a *main objective* (the main story reason for the scene) and *secondary objectives* (to establish a location for the first time; to focus on a specific prop; to establish a character; to hear an important line of dialogue, etc.). These overall objectives (main and secondary) are what drive the film forward and create a state of suspense for the audience.

Tip: If you know the objective and the story points of a scene, you can confidently deal with actors who want to change their dialogue — as long as the change doesn't alter the intent of the scene or the characters.

What is the **central emotional event?** If a script is well written, every scene should have a "central emotional event" (something physical or emotional that happens between the characters), and it's the director's responsibility to make sure all of these emotional events flow together in a cohesive and logical manner.

What are the **obstacles** each character faces in this scene? Obstacles are what stand in the way of a character achieving his or her scene objective. They can be either internal (mental/emotional) or external (physical).

Obstacles continually raise the stakes for your character throughout the story, and they add conflict and tension to the plot by making it harder for the character to achieve their objective. Remember, a good scene should answer these two questions: "What does each character want?" and "Why is he/she having difficulty getting it?"

What are the **scene beats?** To find all the character changes and action events of a scene, you need to break it down into a series of smaller beats (sections or units) — moments in the script when the story suddenly changes direction.

Beats are defined as changes of circumstances or transitions in behavior (think *action–reaction*). Beats usually happen when something changes in the scene, when a new behavior occurs, when another character enters the scene, or when there is a change in direction in the dialogue that creates a change of emotion with one or more of the characters.

The best way to identify a scene beat is to (1) find out where the dialogue subject changes (2) identify any shift in the physical movement of a character (3) determine if a new character enters the scene.

Beats are important because when a director divides a scene into a series of smaller units, they can focus on the details of the scene by using these script beats to develop a blocking plan.

Note: Don't confuse scene beats with character pauses. When a writer wants a character to stop talking and pause for a moment, they write (Beat) by the line of dialogue.

What are the **story points**? These are the elements in any scene (dialogue, action, visuals, sound) that must be made clear to the audience so the story makes sense. (Example: In *Titanic*, Jack *must* win the card game in Act One so he can get onto the ship.)

What are the **plot points**? Plot points are dialogue or action events in every scene that move the story forward.

What creates the **tension**? What story elements in the scene make the audience think, "What will happen next?"

Where is the **climax** of each scene? These don't have to be "big explosions"! They can be small dialogue moments, a certain character reaction, or the reveal of a significant prop.

What are the important **lines of dialogue**? These are lines of dialogue that contain story points the audience must know (and hear clearly) to make sense of a character's actions throughout the rest of the story. (Always look for the facts behind the words or the reality behind a line. In other words, what does a particular line *really* mean?)

Which character **controls** the scene? Which character in the scene drives or pushes the story forward through the use of dialogue or actions?

What is the **conclusion** of the scene? How does the scene end? (Does it set up viewer interest for the next scene? Does it also set up viewer anticipation to see how the film ends?)

Clarity of information. Will this scene improve or confuse the audience's understanding of the overall story? (Do the story points, plot points, action, and dialogue in the scene make sense?)

Here are a few other story elements to look for during your story and scene breakdown:

Counterpoint. Whenever I can, I personally like to add contrasting images (counterpoint) to humanize a character (a bad guy grows flowers and loves his cat) or to make a visual or thematic statement (a funeral on a sunny day or a wedding on rainy day).

Scene transitions. When you analyze a scene you need to think about the "visual entrance cutting point" that takes you into the scene and the "visual exit cutting point" that takes you out of the scene. These "images and/or sounds" are the shots and cuts that "transition" an audience smoothly from one scene into another and from one sequence into another.

Foreshadowing. These are specific images or lines of dialogue in the scene that "subtly foretell" an event that will happen later in the story.

Recurring motifs. These are repeated ideas, patterns, images, sounds, themes, words, etc. that occur throughout the story and reinforce the theme of the film.

Script concerns. What are some potential problem scenes or concerns you have in the script? These are scenes that take usually take longer to set up and shoot because they contain stunts, visual FX, animals, children, or large groups of extras, etc.

9

CHARACTER ANALYSIS

*Every movie, even ensemble pieces (. . .) has to have a lead
character. It has to be about someone. It has to have one or two
main people we can focus our attention on, identify with, and want
to root for — and someone who can carry the movie's theme.
Because liking the person we go on a journey with is the single
most important element in drawing us into the story.*
—BLAKE SNYDER*

CHARACTER BREAKDOWN LIST

After reading the script, making notes about the story structure, and doing your
scene-by-scene analysis, the next part of the director's preproduction homework
is figuring out the development and objectives of the characters through detailed
character analysis.

To find the "heartbeat" of any script, a director needs to understand the "sub-
world" of the characters by exploring their backstories, scene objectives, internal
and external traits, strengths and weaknesses, and relationships with each other.

The first thing you need to do is create a *character breakdown list* for all the
characters in the script who have speaking roles (not extras). List the main characters first and the secondary characters next.

Note: You will eventually use this list to create your character descriptions,
which you give to your casting director before you start auditioning actors.

> If you are directing a TV series, the main characters will already
> be established for you. They are usually numbered "1, 2, 3 . . ." on
> every call sheet.

Save the Cat!: The Last Book on Screenwriting That You'll Ever Need (Michael Wiese
Productions, 2005)

CHARACTER BACKGROUND (PERSONAL HISTORY)

A good screenwriter must fully understand each character's background to dis-cover what "really" motivates their behavior, so a major part of a screenwriter's job is to create a detailed personal history for each character in their script.

These background details include things like physical appearance, personal beliefs, likes and dislikes, daily habits, mental attitudes, childhood experiences, past family history, and significant people and important events in their lives.

As a director, you will never have access to the screenwriter's character back-ground information unless you also wrote the script. But if you did not write the script, I suggest you create simple personal background histories for all your characters to ensure that each character's *behavior remains consistent* throughout the film.

Here are three questions to answer to get you started on your list:
1. What does the writer say about this character? (Scene descriptions)
2. What do other characters say about this character? (Through dialogue)
3. What does the character say about him/herself? (Through inner monologue, dialogue, scene description, narration, etc.)

CHARACTER BACKSTORY (REAL OR IMAGINED EVENTS)

A backstory is an event that has happened in a character's life *right before* the scene started — even if it's the first scene in the film! This moment could have just been shown in the previous scene, or it could be a "made up" off-camera beat just before the scene starts.

A backstory is important for every character because no actor should ever just "enter" a scene. They need to know what they were doing just before the scene starts. The character they are portraying has to come from *some place* and *some event* (big or small) that has just happened to them.

If an actor has a good off-camera beat, when they "enter" the scene the audi-ence should get a feeling they are in the middle of something already happening.

Note: When I say "enter," I don't necessarily mean an actor has to physically walk into the scene. Having a backstory is also necessary for characters who are already present in a scene when it begins.

CHARACTER ARCHETYPES AND THEIR FUNCTIONS

Psychiatrist Carl Jung believed that universal, mythic characters called *archetypes* resided within the collective unconscious of people all over the world (no matter which culture or time period they were born into), and that these archetypes represented the basic *themes* of our experience, ones that evoked deeply emotional responses.

In other words, an archetype is a "commonly accepted image" of a character who personifies a universal pattern of human nature, behavior, and experience. They represent the psychological issues that are uniformly present in all cultures.

Jung also believed that every culture can understand the same basic stories because we *subconsciously* all know what a "hero's journey" is based on: the mythological stories that we have inherited from the past generations of our own cultures.

> The archetypes are representations of psychological issues
> and figures that are universally resonant. Though the physical
> appearance of the archetypes will change, the symbolism behind
> the archetypes has been the same for thousands of years and
> will always remain the same. —WILLIAM INDICK, PH.D.,
> *Psychology for Screenwriters: Building Conflict in Your Script* (Michael
> Wiese Productions, 2004)

So what does all this mean to you?

The use of archetypal characters in a script could help your movie gain universal acceptance because most audiences around the world can subconsciously identify with these characters and their situations within the context of their own cultural and social environments.

However, each archetypal character in your story needs to be believably written as a "real" person so that the audience can instantly identify with them and subconsciously understand their universal dramatic story function.

Each character in a film (or at least the main characters) should have at least one archetypal function or role. It's always helpful for actors to know which archetypes are in their character so they can get more personal insight into the character's specific behaviors and motivations.

There are dozens of archetypes, universal in all human beings, which make up your personality. Here are 10 common archetypal characters and their dramatic functions:

Hero (warrior/soldier): The protagonist or main character of any story.

Villain (outlaw/rebel): The antagonist or main opposition facing the hero.

Love Interest (lover/partner): Object of romantic attraction for the hero.

Mentor (wise old man/expert): A trusted teacher of the hero.

Confidant (sidekick/buddy): The trusted best friend of the hero.

Ruler (boss/queen): An authority figure to the hero.

Jester (fool/clown): Used for humor and comic relief.

Magician (inventor/healer): A visionary person the hero knows or meets.

Caregiver (parent/supporter): A compassionate person the hero meets.

Creator (artist/musician): A creative visionary the hero meets.

Here are 10 more examples of archetypal characters:

The Detective/Sleuth (*Sherlock Holmes*)
The Devil Figure (Captain Hook — *Peter Pan*)
The Initiate (Daniel — *The Karate Kid*)
The Earth Mother (Fairy Godmother — *Cinderella*)
The Temptress (Delilah — *Samson and Delilah*)
The Damsel in Distress (Leticia Musgrove — *Monster's Ball*)
The Star-Crossed Lovers (*Romeo and Juliet*)
The Creature of Nightmare (Sauron — *Lord of the Rings*)
The Regular Person (title character — *Mr. Smith Goes to Washington*)
The Wanderer (title character — *Mad Max* films)

CHARACTER PERSONALITY TRAITS (INTERNAL AND EXTERNAL)

Characterization is a method used by writers to develop a character; they create these by choosing a variety of "personality traits" — including personal appearance, actions, and thoughts — that make fictional characters seem lifelike.

Character traits are the attitudes and behaviors that describe a person's personality. Most personality traits can be discovered by observing how a person acts around you or how they act and respond in certain situations.

Everyone has character traits. Some character traits are good (honest, happy, faithful, devoted, loving, patient) and some character traits are bad (dishonest, rude, greedy, cruel, selfish, angry).

A character's personality traits can also be divided into internal and external categories; they both help shape that character's personality.

Internal character traits describe a person's feelings and they *form* the character by describing their inner motivations, fears, and emotions. (Examples: hopeful, fearless, curious, cheerful, loving)

External character traits describe a person's outside appearance, and they *reveal* the character by describing their physical look, what they do for a living, and where they live. (Examples: tall, thin, wealthy, well-dressed, Canadian)

Because all real people have personality traits (therefore all dramatic characters *must* have personality traits), knowing what type of character you are dealing with is an important first step to understanding the inner world of that character — and that actor!

Analyze each character's personality; this will give you a clear understanding of your characters and what their motivations are, and also help you with the actor's interpretation of the character!

> Make sure the protagonist and antagonist have mostly opposite traits; otherwise, you will have two similar characters who create little or no conflict.

CHARACTER STORY ARCS

By Michael Bruce Adams

> The inner journey tests the hero in the arena of emotions and character, where the hero must learn some lesson or develop some missing aspect of personality. —CHRISTOPHER VOGLER, *The Writer's Journey: Mythic Structure for Writers* (Michael Wiese Productions, 2007)

If we think of plot and character as two sides of the story coin, and we define plot as the results of a character's motivations, decisions, and actions, the *character arc* must then consist of the revelations our character experiences along the journey, the internal transformations motivated by those revelations, and the physical manifestations of those transformations.

Once more, in English . . .

Our heroes are going to enter into situations that provide encounters with others that involve conflict, learning, or both. Those experiences will change those characters, just as all of us are changing and growing with every experience we have.

The changes will inspire a new perspective that can shed light on past events and alter how we view the future. If the perspective change is positive, our heroes might have a more positive and proactive attitude, view future events as opportunities, and carry themselves more uprightly. But if the perspective change is negative, our heroes might take less initiative, view the future with a bit of fear, and slouch as they walk.

As our heroes work through our plotlines, the cumulative internal and external consequences of all those revelations is what we call the transformational arc or character arc . . . the sum total of change the hero experiences from the start of the story to the end.

CHARACTER SUPER-OBJECTIVES, OBJECTIVES, AND ACTIONS

One of the main responsibilities of a director is to help actors achieve a realistic performance. One of the keys to getting a realistic performance is understanding the character's overall story super-objective, their scene objective, and what actions they take to achieve that scene objective.

The *super-objective* (spine) is what the character *NEEDS* most out of life; it is their primal motivation, goal, desire, or dream in the story.

The *scene objective* (goal) is what the character *WANTS* most of all in a scene. This is usually something they want from another person that will help them achieve their overall super-objective.

The *main actions* are what the character DOES (scene action) to get what he/she WANTS (scene objective) to fulfill his/her NEEDS (story super-objective).

For example: if we have an actor playing a *bully* in a film, here's how we could break down the objectives of this character:

Story Super-Objective (Because they *need* to have power over people . . .) What are the main *needs* of the character? What is the *primal motivation* of the character? This is the character's *subtext* (what they really think and feel).

Scene Objective (. . . they *want* to dominate everyone they meet . . .) What does the character *want*? What are his or her *active choices* to achieve the super-objective? This is the character's *text* (what they do).

Main Actions (. . . so this is *what they do* to each person they meet) What the character *does* . . . (Actions) to get what she *wants* . . . (Scene Objective) to fulfill her *needs*! (Super-Objective)

To find out what a character is trying to achieve in a scene, actors must ask (as the character), "*What do I want?*" This specific character objective drives the character through that particular scene.

Opposing Objectives. There would be little drama if characters got what they wanted right away. So as you carry out your script analysis, look carefully at each scene to see if the objectives of the characters cause some sort of conflict, problem, or obstacle for another character.

Before deciding on a character's scene objective, you must know the character's overall story super-objective — their "primal story need," the one thing for which they will sacrifice everything to get what they want.

- What does the character want (more than anything) in this situation?
- Look at the character's behavior. (What he/she does)
- Look at what the character talks about. (What he/she says)
- Look at what happens in the scene and how it ends.
- A character's objective should create obstacles for him or her.
- There should be one main objective per character per scene.
- An objective should be an active choice (a verb) for an actor.
- Strong objectives help actors react to each other, not just "say the lines."
- The simpler the objective, the easier an actor can play it.
- Actors should always play their objective in every scene.

MOTIVATION DETERMINES BEHAVIOR

When it comes to the emotional directing and physical blocking of actors, I believe the three most important words are: *Motivation Determines Behavior*! (*The Oxford Dictionary* [Oxford University Press] defines motivation as "the reason or reasons one has for acting or behaving in a particular way.")

For actors to perform organically and believably, they need to know what *really* motivates their character before they take any action. This motivation will determine how and when actors make movements and say their lines, which will ultimately affect how you block them.

Motivation — Determines — Behavior

Let's break this down:

Motivation (Our inner world)
Determines (Controls)
Behavior (Our outer world)

Now let's break this down even further:

What our needs are (Motivation)
Will decide (Determines)
What action we will take to fulfill our needs (Behavior)

And if we break this down into Super-Objective and Objective:

Motivation: The super-objective (main need) (script subtext)
Determines: Will decide how an actor plays . . . (main actions)
Behavior: The scene objective (what they want) (script text)

In other words, the overall story super-objective of a character will always *influence* how an actor plays his or her scene objective.

⑩

THE 15-STEP SCENE BREAKDOWN SYSTEM

A director makes only one movie in his life. Then he breaks it into pieces and makes it again. — JEAN RENOIR

This *15-Step Scene Breakdown System* is what I use to analyze any script. It takes the most important story and scene elements discussed in this book and organizes them into an easy-to-follow format that takes much of the guesswork out of script analysis. The best way to use this *Breakdown System* is to follow each step in order.

Note: Some of the steps mentioned here are discussed in more detail in the next chapters.

OUTLINE OF 15-STEP SCENE BREAKDOWN SYSTEM

1. What Is the Theme of the Film?
2. What Is the Genre of the Film?
3. What Is the Main Story Question?
4. What Are the Scene Objectives?
5. What Is Each Character's Objective?
6. What Is Each Character's Super-Objective?
7. What Is Each Character's Backstory?
8. Which Character Drives the Scene?
9. What Are Each Character's Scene Actions?
10. Where Are the Scene Beats?
11. Write Out Action Verbs
12. Write Out Images, Comments, and Expressions

13.   Modify Character Dialogue
14.   Write Out Specific Scene Notes
15.   Prepare Shot List/Storyboards/Schematics

DETAILED 15-STEP SCENE BREAKDOWN SYSTEM

1. What Is the Theme of the Film?

The "theme" is the moral, main topic, subject, or concept you are trying to convey to the audience through the text. (*Example*: In *Titanic*, the theme could be "Love Is Everlasting." The sinking of the ship is the dramatic story/plot that supports that theme.)

2. What Is the Genre of the Film?

Genres are types of movies that have identifiable story models and filmic techniques that audiences can easily recognize. (Comedy, crime, action-adventure, horror, fantasy, science-fiction, film noir, western, etc.)

3. What Is the Main Story Question?

There should be one main question presented "indirectly" to the audience in Act One that *must* be answered in Act Three. (In *The Wizard of Oz*, the main question is: "Will Dorothy get back home from Oz?" In *Titanic*, the main question is: "Will Jack and Rose survive the sinking of the ship?")

4. What Are the Scene Objectives?

Every scene in a film has at least *three* purposes: (1) to move the story forward (2) to reveal plot (3) to reveal character. As a director, you need to find the primary story objective (main intent) of the scene by asking: "Why is this scene in the story? What is the main reason for the scene?"

The primary objective of any scene is usually what a character is trying to achieve. It is something the character consciously wants, carrying the actor through his or her scene.

For a director, a scene has a primary objective (the main story reason for the scene) as well as secondary objectives: to establish a location for the first time; to focus on a specific prop; establish a character; to hear an important line of dialogue; etc.

5. What Is Each Character's Scene Objective?

Understanding a character's scene objective is the key to getting a realistic performance from an actor, as well as helping you block and shoot a scene.

A character's scene objective is essentially what the character *wants* most of all in the scene. This is the *text* of the character — the physical world of the character expressed through dialogue or actions.

In a well-written scene, a character's objective should create conflict and obstacles. (HE: Wants to marry her. SHE: Wants to leave the relationship.) A character's scene objective should also be very clear and stated in one simple sentence: "*My objective is to ask Sally to marry me.*"

6. What Is Each Character's Story Super-Objective?

A character's story super-objective is what the character *needs* most in the story. This *subtext* is what your character really thinks or believes — it's the content underneath the dialogue that actors use to show an inner conflict.

What characters are really thinking and feeling has a great effect on why actors move and how they deliver their lines, which leads to believable "magic performance moments."

7. What Is Each Character's Backstory?

A backstory is an event that happened in a character's life before the movie started or *just before* the scene began. This event could have been *shown* in the previous scene, or it could be a "made up" *off-camera beat* just before the scene starts.

8. Which Character Drives the Scene?

Which character in the scene creates an "action" that causes a "reaction" with other characters? Which character says or does something that moves the scene forward? This "controlling" character is the one who drives or pushes the scene toward its conclusion, and it does not have to be the main character.

9. What Are Each Character's Scene Actions?

Every character must be motivated by something before they will take action. Remember: *Motivation (Needs) Determines Behavior (Wants).*

Actions are what a character *does* . . . to get what they *want* . . . to fulfill their *needs*. So look at what a character *does* (their behavior) rather than what they say (their dialogue) to see how they achieve their scene objective.

10. What Are the Scene Beats?

A good way to analyze a scene is by breaking it down into its beats (or units), which are moments in the script when the scene changes direction.

The simplest way to identify a scene beat is by subject (i.e., when a character changes the topic of a conversation). Beat changes can also be identified by specific character movement (i.e., when a new character enters the scene).

By looking at a scene as a series of smaller sections, the director can focus on the details to develop a rough blocking plan, figure out the shots, and give direction to actors on set.

11. Write Out Action Verbs

In order to perform any scene convincingly, an actor needs to find the right action to fit a particular situation or line of dialogue. *Action verbs* are words that express a specific emotion or action, and they have an emotional effect on another person that anyone can understand (i.e., to attack, to influence, to harass, to startle, to question, to invite, to demand).

By using action verbs, an actor can concentrate completely on the situation and his scene objectives. A verb gives them a clear *motivation*, which they need to make their character come alive.

Actors need actions because it is difficult to "act" adjectives. So instead of asking an actor to be *sexy* (a result) ask the actor to *flirt* or to *seduce* the other actor. This encourages the actor to engage emotionally with the other actor rather than just focusing on trying to be sexy.

12. Write Out Images, Comments, and Expressions

The value of having a script read-through and actor rehearsals is that you will discover certain scenes or lines of dialogue that may give the actors trouble or confuse them when they are on the set.

So another valuable part of your scene breakdown is to write out relevant *images* or *visualizations* that you can share with the actors if they need help clarifying their scene objective, if they stumble over specific lines, or if they are having trouble achieving an emotional beat.

Write down specific *comments* that seem appropriate for each scene (like script facts, location issues, camera movements) as well as certain *expressions* (*What would you feel like if a puppy licked your face?*) that you can tell an actor to help them achieve a specific emotional beat.

13. Write Out Specific Scene Notes

This is where you make specific notes on the margins of your script regarding important production elements, specific shots, camera movements, sound-design elements, location issues, or edits to a scene.

For example: During a specific line of dialogue you may want a curtain to start moving behind an actor, so you make a note for your special-effects department. Or you may want to block-shoot two scenes that occur on different script days, so you make a note for the wardrobe department.

14. Modifying Character Dialogue

I'm a firm believer in the rule "Less is more!" As the director, it's your responsibility to take a written document (the script) and translate it into a visual format (film or video). This means you may want to use appropriate visuals instead of certain lines of dialogue to make a story point or to show what an actor is thinking.

Remember: It's always better to *show* the audience what a character is thinking rather than have them talk about it. ("Motion" pictures!) So after you have done all your script, scene, and character-analysis breakdowns, make another pass at the script to see what dialogue can be altered, reduced, or omitted by using visuals (and/or sound) to get your points across.

Note: On a television series, the producers are usually the writers, and they are sometimes hesitant to have any dialogue changed or removed. But if you have done your script-analysis breakdown and can show them that your ideas will make the scene visually better, go for it — they can only say no!

15. Prepare Shot Lists, Storyboards, and Schematics

After you do all 14 script-analysis steps, you can now figure out how to shoot every scene.

A *shot list* is a description of all the camera angles for a scene and include shot size, camera movement, character movement, and coverage. Shot lists should be mandatory for every director because they guide you through the blocking and shooting processes. They are also extremely helpful for your 1st AD and DOP.

Note: Again, like a roadmap, a shot list may give you a path to your destination, but you might not always be able to follow it. Changes will happen on the set that you did not anticipate, so you need to remain open-minded and be ready to alter your shooting plan to fit any new situation that occurs.

A *storyboard* is a series of sequential images of a scene or a sequence. Storyboards are primarily used to help film directors previsualize scenes which contain complicated actor blocking, action sequences, or layers of visual effects.

A *schematic* is a diagram of how the director wants to block a scene and where the camera will be placed. It is drawn from a high angle and gives a "bird's eye view" of the set.

As a director you may want to fully storyboard each scene in your film (even scenes with two people sitting at a table) so you have the final product in mind when you shoot.

But remember: Due to location logistics, lighting requirements, and actor changes, storyboards and schematics (whether they're done simply on paper or through detailed computer programs) will never fully duplicate what happens on a real set.

So please use your shot lists, storyboards, and schematics as good production guides. When you're focused and in the moment on set, you will have the opportunity to discover better blocking scenarios, better camera angles, and magic performance moments that you never would have thought about sitting at home writing out your shots and storyboards.

11

DIRECTING THE VISUAL CONCEPT

A style is not a matter of camera angles or fancy
footwork, it's an expression, an accurate expression
of your particular opinion. —KAREL REISZ

THE DIRECTOR'S VISUAL CONCEPT

The director's *visual concept* is the image structure or visual style of the "words written in a script." It's your visual approach to the plot and themes of the film through the specific use of light, shadow, colors, composition, lens, angles, focus, depth, movement, pacing, narrative structure, symbols, sounds, music, montage, casting, locations, hair, makeup, costumes, set dressing, props, etc.

A director's *visual style* is often an expression of their personality; it shapes the look and feel of a film. When we think of visual style, certain directors will always come to mind because of their use of distinctive themes or "visual signatures" that appear throughout most of their work (i.e., John Ford, Tim Burton, Wes Anderson, Zhang Yimou, Sergio Leone, Akira Kurosawa, Terrence Malick).

CREATING THE DIRECTOR'S VISUAL CONCEPT

Before you can fully bring any script to life, you first need to research every available source (movies, books, magazines, plays, paintings, television, internet, locations, music, etc.) that will immerse you in the *outer story world* (plot, actions, events, characters, text) and the *inner story world* (story themes, character subtext, and inner feelings you want to arouse in the audience).

General Research

The audience should always learn something new from watching your film: about the characters, about the location, about the time period. So ask yourself, "What do I want the audience to know? What do I want the audience to feel? What do I want the audience to experience?" In other words, ascertain what emotion or feeling you want the audience to have in a scene, then find ways to achieve it.

You need to keep true to the "story rules" of your specific film world by managing the unique characteristics of the story to create a film that is believable. Remember, even fantasy and science-fiction films have to be "believable" within the realm of their particular "unreal" world.

Create a world in which the characters are in conflict. Understand your characters' behavior. What are their motives in every scene? This will affect their actions and what they do as a result.

Find out what generates the scene action before it happens. What event in the scene begins the action? What motivates a character to take action? (It could be an event, a line of dialogue, or a certain character's look.)

What do your characters really want? Develop the subtext (through dialogue and actions) to make it believable by discovering what the character is really trying to say — and why!

Use counterpoint to create multidimensional characters. Unless a person is certifiably insane, everyone has the capacity to love one person deeply and hate another person or group just as passionately.

Everyone has secret lives and fantasies. What are yours? What are they for your characters?

Specific Research

What is the audience is going to *see*? Since you decide where to place the camera, you determine what the audience is going to see — and not see.

What are the *tone* and *mood* of the film? What do you want the audience to feel? (Light or dark? Warm or cold? Comedic or dramatic? Sensual or sexual? Serious or satirical?)

What is the *pacing* of the story? What is the pace at the beginning of the film? What is the pace at the end of the film? (Fast-paced action sequences, lengthy dialogue sequences, long scenic-transition shots, etc.)

Is there one *main image* used to take the audience into this story world? (In *Empire of the Sun*, Spielberg used the sun as his main image, represented most clearly by the Japanese flag.)

Design a *visual motif*, images or symbols that establish a certain mood. When you repeat a motif, it becomes a stylistic image pattern that develops a theme or character over the entire film.

What is the *first scene or image* in your film? (What images will grab the audience and take them into your world?)

What is the *last scene or image* in your film? (What do you want the audience to feel at the end of the movie?)

What *dialogue* is the most important to be heard? (Know your story points.)

What is the *rhythm* of each scene? Every scene should have highs and lows, so graph out the rhythm of each scene to see what the whole film looks like. (If you graph out a scene and it looks like the flatline of a hospital EKG monitor, that's exactly what your audience may feel — nothing!)

COLLABORATING WITH THE PRODUCTION DESIGNER AND DOP

One of the first meetings the director has with the production designer and director of photography is the *creative concept meeting*. Together they decide on the tone, look, mood, and feel of the film.

The production designer then creates a "mood board" (a collage of various images, colors, materials, objects, text, etc.) that all departments can use to help them visually illustrate the look and tone of the film.

The director of photography now has a clear vision of how the movie looks so he/she can create a *visual image system* (through lighting, composition, camera angles, depth of field, colors, locations, etc.) that will convey the director's message to the audience.

The DOP and production designer also work closely with the director on the design and building of any sets, as well as scouting for locations that perfectly fit the visual concept and style of the film.

SHOOTING PLOT (LENS PLOT)

One of the things you need to do with your DOP is design your *"shooting plot or lens plot,"* which is a stylistic camera plan that makes a "subtextual visual comment" across the entire film. This can be as simple as choosing which lenses you want for a particular scene to determining the height of the camera you want to use for each character in different scenes.

For example, in one sequence you may want to start with a wide lens to establish all the characters having a discussion around a table. As the film progresses and the story gets more intense, you start using progressively longer lenses to separate the characters and create more tension.

Likewise, you can start the same table discussion scenes with the camera at eye level for all the characters. As the film progresses and the story gets more dramatic, you gradually raise or lower the camera for specific characters, depending on whether they are in a position of power or not.

VISUAL CONCEPT EXAMPLES

Patterns (Symbolic Meanings)
- Triangles (female, relationships, romance)
- Squares (trapped, rigid, conservative)
- Circles (infinity, without beginning or end)
- Horizontal lines (level, true, balanced, passive)
- Vertical lines (firm, upward, climbing, active, trapped)

Motion (Reading *left to right*)
- Motion left to right feels comfortable, natural, going somewhere, finishing.
- Motion right to left has a feeling of conflict, evil, trouble, coming back.
- (Could have the opposite feelings for those cultures who read *right to left*.)

Focus (Movement vs. Stillness)

- Movement creates focus. (We notice a moving person in a still crowd.)
- Stillness creates focus. (We notice a still person in a moving crowd.)

Balance (Composition)

- Balanced images (stability, fairness, calmness)
- Unbalanced images (shakiness, instability, conflict, tension)
- Centered images (making no statement, intelligence, calmness)
- Off-center images (implied action, entering or leaving)

SYMBOLIC MEANINGS OF COLORS

What is the thematic color of your story? What is the color of each scene? What are the colors of each character? All colors mean something on an emotional level, and they can add additional *visual subtextual layers* to your film — depending on the *context* they are used for in a scene. For example:

WARM COLORS (red, yellow, orange) can be *pleasing & joyful* OR *aggressive & violent*.

COOL COLORS (blue, green, white) can be *comforting & calming* OR *cold & impersonal*.

Here are some basic psychological and emotional meanings of 12 colors:

Primary Colors

Red — anger, passion, rage, desire, excitement, energy, speed, strength, power, heat, love, aggression, danger, fire, blood, war, violence

Yellow — wisdom, knowledge, relaxation, joy, happiness, optimism, idealism, imagination, hope, sunshine, summer, dishonesty, cowardice, betrayal, jealousy, deceit, illness, hazard

Blue — faith, spirituality, loyalty, fulfillment, peace, tranquility, calm, stability, harmony, unity, trust, truth, confidence, security, order, sky, water, cold, technology, depression

Secondary Colors
Orange — humor, energy, balance, warmth, enthusiasm, vibrant, expansive, flamboyant

Purple — erotic, royalty, nobility, spirituality, ceremony, mysterious, transformation, wisdom, enlightenment, cruelty, arrogance, mourning, power, sensitive, intimacy

Green — healing, soothing, perseverance, tenacity, self-awareness, proud, unchanging nature, environment, healthy, good luck, renewal, youth, vigor, spring, generosity, fertility, jealousy, inexperience, envy

Other Colors
Black — no, power, sexuality, sophistication, formality, elegance, wealth, mystery, fear, anonymity, unhappiness, depth, style, evil, sadness, remorse, anger, death

White — yes, protection, love, reverence, purity, simplicity, cleanliness, peace, humility, precision, innocence, youth, birth, winter, snow, good, sterility, marriage, death (Eastern cultures), cold, clinical, sterile

Grey — neutral, uncommitted, insulated, noninvolvement, security, reliability, intelligence, staid, modesty, dignity, maturity, solid, conservative, practical, sadness, boring, old age

Brown — materialistic, sensation, earth, home, outdoors, reliability, comfort, endurance, stability, simplicity

Silver — riches, glamorous, distinguished, earthy, natural, sleek, elegant, high-tech

Gold — precious, riches, extravagance, warm, wealth, prosperity, grandeur

Character-Type Colors

Colors can also be used to represent certain qualities of a character.

Red, orange, magenta
(Characters who interact with their physical environment.)

Blue, violet, lavender, crystal
(Characters who live in a spiritual world.)

Bright colors such as orange, yellow, red, light green, light blue
(Characters with good physical, mental, and emotional health.)

Muddy colors such as brown, black, dark green, dark blue
(Characters with depression, anger, self-pity.)

Warm colors such as red, orange, yellow
(Extroverted characters who are outgoing, friendly, and sociable.)

Cool colors such as green, blue, purple
(Introverted characters who are loners, withdrawn, and weird.)

> It's essential you learn what certain colors mean to various cultures and traditions around the world. For example, in Western cultures black is the color of mourning, but in some Eastern cultures white is the color of mourning.

12

THE DIRECTOR/
ACTOR RELATIONSHIP

*I actually think if people are like . . . knowing about my
movies thirty or fifty years from now it's gonna be because
of the characters that I created. And I really only got
one chance to get it right. I have to cast the right people
to make those characters come alive and hopefully
live for a long time.* —QUENTIN TARANTINO*

FAMOUS DIRECTOR/ACTOR RELATIONSHIPS

The importance of the director/actor relationship is a crucial element of the filmmaking process. If the actor and director do not connect creatively or personally,
differences of opinion will be difficult to resolve, personalities will clash, and performances will suffer.

However, an actor and director trusting each other and working together creatively to get layered and believable performances can create magic on the screen.
Here are some examples of famous director/actor relationships:

John Ford & John Wayne; Akira Kurosawa & Toshiro Mifune; Tim Burton
& Helena Bonham Carter and Johnny Depp; Martin Scorsese & Robert De
Niro; Ingmar Bergman & Liv Ullmann and Max von Sydow; François Truffaut
& Jean-Pierre Léaud.

---

*From his 2013 Oscar speech for *Django Unchained*

10 STAGES OF THE DIRECTOR/ACTOR WORKING RELATIONSHIP

The following list is a basic breakdown of the director's working relationship with an actor during the production of most films, which starts in the first casting session and ends in the ADR session.

Your interactions with an actor may be affected by your relationship with them. For example, if you are casting experienced actors for a role in your film, how *you* perform during the first audition will have a bearing on how each actor reacts through the remaining stages.

1. The Audition (First Interview)
2. Casting Callbacks (Several)
3. Screen Tests (Optional)
4. Actor Interviews/Meetings (Optional)
5. Script Read-Through
6. Cast Rehearsals (Several)
7. On Set (Blocking)
8. On Set (Rehearsals)
9. On Set (Shooting)
10. ADR Sessions

Note: You may have more of these stages (actor/director meetings; reshoots after principal photography) or you may have fewer (no time for rehearsals; no money left for ADR).

BUILDING TRUST

What actors want most from their relationship with a director is *TRUST*! Actors usually begin a film fully trusting the director; it's up to the director to keep (or lose) that trust!

All good relationships are built on trust. Trust means we have confidence in a person because we believe they are truthful and reliable. Trusting someone completely is always a commitment of faith, especially if we need to feel emotionally and physically safe. Without trust we lose our faith and confidence in a person.

We can no longer believe them, and we can never truly feel safe or vulnerable with that person again.

Good actors will quite often take their time before they decide they can trust you. If an actor feels the director can't be trusted to know a good performance from a bad one, he or she will watch his own performance and start to direct himself, ultimately becoming "*director proof.*"

So how do you get actors to trust you?

Actors want a director who can listen to them because they are focused on one thing: the role they are playing. To be believable, an actor must surrender completely to feelings and impulses. Good directors understand an actor's vulnerability, and will always create a physically and emotionally safe place for them to perform.

THE 5 GROUPS OF ON-CAMERA PERFORMERS

Actors are not the only ones who "perform" on camera. The following is a list of other on-camera talent you will deal with on most film productions. These 5 groups are not based just on union descriptions, but also my own experiences of how each group *functions* on a film set.

Actors

Here are eight categories of actors you could work with. By "categories," I mean how each group fits into the hierarchy and politics of our business. Each group has a different share of the power on a set.

- The legend (Jerry Lewis, Lauren Bacall, Tony Curtis)
- The movie star (Tom Hanks, Robert De Niro, Julia Roberts)
- The television star (Carol Burnett, Jerry Seinfeld, Tim Allen)
- The crossover star (TV to film) (George Clooney, Will Smith)
- The crossover star (film to TV) (Judy Davis, Glenn Close)
- The guest star (Brad Pitt on *Friends*, Sally Field on *ER*)
- The principal actor (larger speaking roles)
- The day player (smaller speaking roles)

Stunt performers

Stunt performers perform the harder and more dangerous action for movies and television. Here are the 3 basic categories they fall under:

- Stunt actor (Plays a character — could have dialogue)
- Stunt performer (Not a specific character — no dialogue)
- Stunt double (Takes the place of actors for more dangerous stunts)

Background performers

Background performers are also known as extras or atmosphere. I have broken this group into 3 categories. (The last one is my own special category; they are paid the same as general extras.)

- Special-skills extras — They have a special skill or ability they have practiced and trained for. (Football players, scuba divers, ballroom dancers.)
- General extras — These are the majority of extras on a film set. (Crowd on street, passengers on a plane, bar patrons, students in school hallway.)
- "Uniformed" extras — They portray background characters the audience knows something about. (Police, waiters, nurses, military, firefighters.)

Actor photo doubles

Photo doubles "take the place of" an actor on camera when the actor's face is not seen. They are matched for body size, skin color, hair, and physical movement. They are used mostly for second units and splinter units (car drive-bys, etc.) and are also used as body doubles for love scenes and nude scenes. They can also be used by the main unit if an actor is not available for wide shots or over-the-shoulder shots, etc.

Stand-ins

Although stand-ins (second team) are not technically "performers," I have included them here because of the invaluable role they play on any film set.

Stand-ins are not hired to work for the actors; they work for the director of photography — to "stand in place of the actors" while the DOP lights them. The camera crew also uses stand-ins for rehearsing camera movement and focus during the lighting process.

On larger movies, stand-ins are picked by the DOP after the major cast has been chosen, although some big-name actors could have their own stand-ins they prefer the DOP to use.

TIP: On many low-budget productions, producers do not have the money for stand-ins. But if they can budget for at least two experienced stand-ins, you will save some relighting time when the cast arrives back on set for the camera rehearsal — which means a few more camera setups for you during the day!

15 ACTING WORDS AND PHRASES FOR DIRECTORS

Actors need to TRUST you because they rely on the director to help them create sustained and believable performances. One of the keys to getting successful performances from actors is *good communication* between the director and the actor.

For many first-time directors, working with experienced actors can be frustrating and intimidating because the actor's world is filled with many strange and scary words like *character spine, action verbs, objectives, obstacles, permission, in the moment, improvisation, and motivation*!

And this dilemma doesn't just apply to first-time directors. There are many experienced directors today who are more comfortable working with the "mechanics" of filmmaking than working intimately with actors on their performances. These directors feel safer with the crew because their discussions are mostly about objective technical issues.

So if you can't direct actors in a language they can understand, many actors will slowly lose faith in you and start to direct themselves. They do this not out of spite or ego, but to *protect* themselves and their craft!

Remember, when it comes to communicating with actors, a director can be either part of the solution or part of the problem! So if you don't know how to speak the actors' language, you could have a difficult time getting actors to trust you. Without trust, you may have a challenging time blocking with them and getting layered performances from them.

To help you better communicate with actors, here are 15 key "acting" words and phrases used in both film and theatre.

1. Action verbs

Action verbs are words that stimulate specific emotions because they express an "action" anyone can *do*. For example: to accuse, to control, to seduce, to flirt, to ignore, to flaunt, to berate, etc. And if you want to increase (or decrease) the intensity of a line, you can change the actor's intention by changing the verb.

For example, you told an actor: "Go to Sally and *plead* with her to tell you her secret," but the performance was not strong enough for the scene. So now you could say, "Go to Sally and *demand* that she tell you her secret." And if you really need to raise the stakes, you could say, "Go to Sally and *threaten* her if she doesn't tell you her secret."

2. Characterization

For actors to be completely comfortable inhabiting the actions and language of their characters, they take what is written in the script and add more layers to create a total believable life for their characters. They do this by exploring the two factors that shape each character: the *internal* factors which *form* character (feelings/emotions) and the *external* factors which *reveal* character (car/clothes/house).

3. Emotional memory (also Sense memory)

Emotional memory (also called emotional recall or affective memory) is an acting technique created by *Constantin Stanislavski that re-creates a real emotional or psychological moment of a past event that actually happened to the actor to help them realistically portray a character's emotions on stage.

When an actor uses this technique, they remember a past experience (as if it is occurring at the present time), which then helps them to create a believable emotion their character would actually be experiencing at that moment.

Example: An actress is looking at the actor playing her father lying in a coffin and has to feel real grief over his "death." However, in real life she has never had anyone in her family or a close friend die. So to attain a believable feeling of grief for this scene, she remembered when her cat was run over by a car. She then

---

*Constantin Stanislavski, *An Actor Prepares* (Theatre Arts Books, 1936)

brought up the *real emotions of grief* she felt back then and used them in this scene.

Sense memory is another emotional memory technique that involves remembering an experience from our 5 main senses (touch, taste, smell, sight, sound) to create a genuine emotional reaction to a specific moment in a scene.

4. Given circumstances

Given circumstances are the facts in a script the writer has provided about the plot, characters, costumes, props, conditions of life, time period, locations, etc. For the actor, a given circumstance is also information about who they are, what they are doing, and why they are doing it.

5. Improvisation

Improvisation is the art of acting and reacting to one's surroundings "in the moment." It's an essential component of the actor's training, and is a particularly useful technique for helping actors focus and concentrate.

So when actors are having a difficult time understanding or relating to a scene, give them some time to improvise. It loosens them up and gives them the freedom to find the real meaning (subtext) of the lines and the scene.

Improvisation also gives you a chance to discover something you may have missed in the scene, and also lets you see if the actors are on the same page.

6. In the moment

Reacting *in the moment* means actors are totally present with both the text and their scene partners and not thinking about their next line or next action.

This technique creates powerful performances because when actors are not worried about their blocking or their next line, they will *instinctively react* and be completely immersed in their scene.

A good way for a director to help an actor's performance is to make sure they are always listening *in the moment* to the other actors in the scene. If this happens, then every take will be a little different because they are reacting to the other actor "as if for the first time."

Remember, an actor always knows their character's destiny, but the character they are playing does not. So it is up to the director to make sure the actor is always *in the moment* and does nothing to foreshadow or give away anything that will happen to their character.

THE DIRECTOR/ACTOR RELATIONSHIP

7. Inciting incident

The inciting incident is the event or decision in Act One when the hero encounters the problem or challenge that will force them to go on a "hero's journey," changing their life forever. In Joseph Campbell's 3-act structure outline of the hero's journey, the inciting incident is known as the "call to adventure."

8. Indicating

A common problem for some actors is the temptation to indicate (reveal physically) an emotional beat they are not actually feeling by showing the audience something about the character through their acting. Most people call this kind of performance overacting — I call it "face acting"!

When an actor is not feeling a specific emotion, they may *indicate* the desired emotion by "acting" that feeling without being connected truthfully to the emotion. So make sure your actors *don't play the result* of what they want the audience to feel. (See #14 below.)

Remember, "close-ups don't lie" because the camera won't let you get away with anything — especially when it comes to faking emotions.

9. Italian reading

An Italian reading is when actors recite their dialogue very quickly without pauses several times in a row. This technique is used very often in theatre to help actors get ready before they go on stage.

On a film set you can use Italian readings when actors are tired, forgetting their lines, anticipating the next line, or to increase the pace of the scene. The objective here is to get the actors "out of their heads" (not thinking about their lines) and back into their bodies (listening and feeling).

10. Magic if (As if)

The magic "as if" is another acting technique created by Constantin Stanislavski.*
Rather than attempting to believe they really are the character, actors can play "as if" they (the actor) were in the same situation as the character in the scene.

In other words, when actors are performing on a film set, they ask themselves, "If this 'story' environment were real, how would I (the actor) react? What would

---

*Constantin Stanislavski, *An Actor Prepares* (Theatre Arts Books, 1936)

I (the actor) do?" This creates a real inner activity and makes their performances more realistic.

11. On the nose
When you see an actor "acting the character" instead of "being the character," it usually means they are performing "from their head" and not reacting in the moment. In other words, they fail to connect believably with their character because they don't understand the subtext of the scene.

When this happens to inexperienced or nervous actors, they are usually just trying to remember their lines, which causes them to literally "recite" the text without feeling or emotion. This makes their performance too "on the nose."

12. Pacing
From an actor's point of view, the pacing of a scene is the speed at which they pick up their cues and deliver their next line. Every script will have slow-paced and fast-paced dialogue scenes. It's *up to the director* to match the actor pacing of those scenes with the editing tempo and rhythm of the film itself (i.e., the director's visual concept for the film).

In all my years of teaching and critiquing literally hundreds of short film "director cuts," I consistently found that most new directors allowed their actors to speak at a slower pace, even if a scene was meant to be fast. Only rarely did I witness actors picking up their cues and overlapping their dialogue, mainly because they were experienced film actors.

The main reason these student directors did not interfere with the pacing of the actors was simple — they did not have enough set experience directing actors to understand how "actor dialogue pacing" affected the overall rhythm and tempo of a scene. It's only when they got to the editing room that they saw the problem. If they had been smart enough to shoot good coverage, they could usually fix the actor pacing in the scene.

13. Permission
Permission is a powerful performance tool. When you give an actor permission to "take risks and not be perfect" (without being judged), you will both have an opportunity to find new insights into the character and discover unexpected "magic performance moments."

So if actors have a problem remembering their lines, connecting with their characters, or finding the subtext of a scene, take a few minutes and give them permission to freely explore their characters by trying crazy ideas or improvising dialogue and actions. But you must never make any judgments! Just allow them the freedom to play and create in a safe place. (This is also a good way for a director to gain the trust of the actors!)

14. Result directing

If I asked you right now *to be very angry*, what would you do? How would you *behave*? How would you *show* your anger? How would you *act* angry?

This type of direction is called "directing for results": telling the actor what to feel, how to move, and how to react — without giving them any clues as to why or how. Result directing takes the actor's concentration off his acting partner as he "goes into his head" (he is no longer in the moment) and starts thinking if he is as "angry" as you want him to be.

Examples of result directing are: *"I want you to shout . . . to cry now . . . to laugh louder . . . to be sad . . . to be happy . . . to pick up your pen on this line . . ."*

The main reason result direction doesn't work very well is that "all emotions have a different way of being expressed." So if you give the same result direction (*be sad*) to five different actors, they will all express that emotion a little differently.

Remember, all emotions are the result of an actor's needs and wants. These emotional responses come as a consequence of the actor trying to achieve their scene objective. Good directing is searching for the right words (action verbs, facts, anecdotes, images) to find more powerful ways to help actors identify their scene objective, create motivated actions, and naturally feel the emotions you are after.

Tip: When you use a lot of result direction on experienced actors, some of them may decide you don't know how to direct and slowly lose faith in you. (Remember: Trust!) However, there are some actors who only want you to give them result-based direction. These actors will always be able to laugh, get angry, or cry right on cue, but be careful because some of those performances may not have the most subtle acting you will see!

15. Spine (also Through-line/Super-objective)

The spine of a script is the reason or main purpose of the character's journey. It's what the hero wants more than anything, and the main character's spine is usually linked to the central theme of the script.

For example: In the first Jason Bourne film, what was the spine of the movie? In other words, what was the story really about (story spine/theme) and what did Jason Bourne want (character spine/super-objective)? Answer: To discover his identity. To find out who he really was — and that was what the audience wanted to find out as well.

In any film, a character should have only one spine for the whole story. To find a specific character's spine, look for the main character's transforming event and its end result.

When thinking of a film's spine, think of our body's spine and its purpose. Quite simply, the spine "links" or "holds" the story (the body) together. And what happens when one of the links is out of place? You get a disjointed story — and a pain the back!

Note: I first picked up Judith Weston's book *Directing Actors** shortly after it was published, and it very quickly became my "bible" for working with actors. Even today, I reread her book to refresh my directing-actor skills; the content of her book will always remain "evergreen." I strongly suggest you get a copy Judith's book for your library.

courtesy John Weston

Peter and Judith Weston

---

*Judith Weston, *Directing Actors: Creating Memorable Performances for Film & Television* (Michael Wiese Productions, 1996), mwp.com

13

PREPARING FOR THE CASTING SESSION

An audition is not a performance. Auditioning and performing are two separate skills. Many actors have both skills, but there are actors who audition well and don't work well. There are also actors who work well and are great in performance, but who don't audition well. Which kind of actor would you rather have in your movie or TV show? —JUDITH WESTON*

After sitting in dozens of casting sessions as a director and producer, as well as spending hundreds of hours teaching indie filmmakers and students how to audition actors, I have witnessed "the good, the bad, and the ugly" of the casting process.

Like everything else in the film business, "there are no rules (in casting), only opinions," so in these next two chapters I'm going to give you my well-researched "opinion" on how to conduct and control your casting sessions to best discover the right actors for each role in your film.

GETTING READY FOR YOUR FIRST CASTING SESSION

In her book *Casting Revealed: A Guide for Film Directors*, 2nd edition (Routledge Press, 2016), Hester Schell defines casting as "the *process* of finding the best roles in your movie" and audition as "the *job interview* used during the casting process."

---

*Directing Actors: Creating Memorable Performances for Film & Television (Michael Wiese Productions, 1999)

Early in prep you will have a meeting with the producer and the casting director to share your ideas about the characters. This is an important meeting because it's where you find out if you and the producer have similar casting ideas. (Remember, if you are directing television, it's the producer's show and they have final say on everything — including casting!)

After this meeting, the casting director puts together a *first-look list* of actors that fit the character traits and specific looks discussed in the meeting with the producer. He or she then schedules her own closed casting sessions (without the director and producer) and makes a "short list" of actors for you and the producer to watch on video. After you and the producer have viewed the short list, you send the casting director a list of actors you want to audition. He or she will then schedule a series of live casting sessions.

> If you are working on a television series you might only be casting from these and subsequent videos — and never end up in a live casting session.

And then this scenario happens: You arrive at the casting session with the producer (usually late because you were scouting locations) and you meet the casting director who introduces you to the videographer (who records the actors on camera) and the reader (who's hopefully an actor who reads the script with the auditioning actors).

You are then handed a long list of all the auditioning actors and the roles they are reading for. The first actor enters, slates for the camera, and does their first read. You give them an objective adjustment, and they do the second reading. After they leave, you quickly make your evaluation notes and the next actor walks in. Wash, rinse, repeat!

And when the casting session is finished, you have a headache, the producer doesn't agree with any actor you like, the casting director is already setting up another session, and there's a message from the office informing you of a complete revision of the script waiting for you when you get back!

But let's back up for a moment!

If you're reading this book, you are probably a film student, an independent low-budget filmmaker, or a film-industry professional interested in directing, AND you likely don't have very much money to make your movie!

So if you are making a student film, directing a short film, or are an unknown director making your first low-budget indie film, honestly answer this important question before scheduling your first casting session: "Why would any actor want to audition for my film if it's NOT for the money — or the craft service?"

The answer is pretty simple. Actors want to audition for you because they want *to work on an interesting story*; they want *to play a character that has depth*; they want *to get more on-set experience*; they want *to get clips for their demo reel*; and they want *to meet industry people and make contacts*.

LOOKING FOR ACTORS "BELOW THE TIP OF THE ICEBERG"

If you are an experienced director with a few good films under your belt, you will probably be able to attract well-known and experienced actors to your casting sessions and hire many of them for your projects.

But what if you are an "unknown," low-budget indie director, or you just direct short films on the weekends? How are you going to find the best actors for your project when you are not able to attract (or pay) for the most experienced actors?

Well, don't fear! If you can't attract (or afford) the most experienced actors to your casting sessions, there are dozens of undiscovered talented actors who could be right for a part in your film — as long as you know *how* to attract them and *how* to effectively audition them!

Unfortunately, many of these "undiscovered actors" are rarely given the chance to have a good audition. This prevents them from securing future auditions — which stops them from getting experience — which stops you from auditioning them. But this dilemma can be solved once you know how to effectively discover and audition the majority of actors who remain "below the tip of the iceberg."

CREATING "TARGETED" CHARACTER DESCRIPTIONS

Before you start auditioning, attract the "best qualified" actors to your casting sessions by creating a *casting breakdown* sheet that contains: the film synopsis, a short description of each character, casting dates/times, and the casting location. You can also add tentative shoot dates, union or non-union roles, pay rates, and any other information about your film that would attract the right actors to your audition. (Shooting out of town, winter locations, working nights, must be able to ride a horse, etc.)

As you (or your casting director or producer) create the casting breakdowns, please think of them as *"casting marketing tools"* because you want to create a "well-targeted advertisement" to attract the right actors to audition for each role. And one of the most important creative details of your casting breakdown is how you write the *character descriptions* for each character in your film.

Most character descriptions that I have read describe primarily the external or "outside life" of the character. While there are certain physical features that are essential for most characters, it's important to understand that outer traits (ethnicity, height, weight, hair color, etc.) are *not always* necessary for every character — especially for your secondary roles.

Here are two simple "external" character descriptions:

[JOHN] Caucasian. 45 years old. Dishwasher. Balding & thin. Limps. Lives at home with his parents. Wants to play the violin professionally.

[MARY] African-American. 25 years old. University student. Pretty and vivacious. Needs to lose some weight. Struggles to accept her female side in a man's world.

Firstly, you should recognize that most of the character qualities described above are the outer traits of the character. When casting, *remain open* to actors who give you a great reading of the role but do not look exactly like the character you had envisioned.

In fact, a lot of movie roles have been created by actively *casting against type*. Even the sex of a secondary character could change because of an interesting read during an audition. So a character described as a "55-year-old male judge" could easily be turned into a "60-year-old female judge."

"Internal" character descriptions explain the essential physical and background information about the character as well, but they also show a glimpse into the character's inner life, which adds depth and offers valuable insight into the role for the benefit of your potential actors.

Here are the same two "external" character descriptions with some added "internal" traits:

[JOHN] Caucasian. 45 years old. Dishwasher who limps from a car accident when he was 7. He is passionate about classical music, and he dreams of playing his violin in an orchestra. He lives at home with his mother and stepfather, who abused him when he was a child.

[MARY] African-American. 25 years old. Vivacious university student studying engineering. She grew up with three older brothers who always bullied her. She constantly pushes herself to be the best in a man's world while struggling to accept her emotional, female side.

In the descriptions above, you can immediately see the character you're describing, but you are not confining that character to specific physical characteristics.

By adding subtext (and inner conflict) to your character descriptions, you can attract more experienced, better prepared actors to your auditions. (Remember all the different reasons why actors want to audition for a film!)

Of course, specific physical qualities may be necessary for certain characters, and you need to mention these in your casting breakdown. For example, if special skills are required for the role, like the ability to ride a bike or swim, then those skills need to be added. Similarly, you'll want to specify if it's integral to the story that two characters look physically related (like a brother and sister or parents and children).

It's also important to note if there are any unique physical demands, violence, implied nudity, and/or sexuality in the role. In short, know what you absolutely need in a character and *remain flexible* about what you don't to tell a story.

To review: Good character descriptions should have two parts to them:

1. *Text*: Describe the "outer life" of the character. (Age, general description, what they do for a living, etc.)

2. *Subtext*: Describe some part of the "inner life" of the character. (What is really going on inside of them? What conflicts do they have?)

Remember, your character descriptions need to be "casting marketing tools" used to attract the most qualified actors in your area. By using subtext to create an "inner emotional conflict," you achieve depth within the character to "target" those potential actors.

THE 6 STAGES OF CASTING ACTORS

Actors need to be vulnerable in order to express their deepest emotions, which is why trust is what actors need most from a director — and this trust starts with the very first casting session!

How your auditions and callbacks are organized and run by the casting director (or the producer on low-budget shows) is a very important part of the casting process. What follows is a proven step-by-step casting process you can follow and adapt to fit your personal style and situation.

> The casting process I'm about to discuss is not a new concept, and many experienced film and TV directors use a variation of this process every day. Since I first started casting actors as a television director in the 1980s (as well as my years of experience teaching filmmakers and actors worldwide), I have seen over and over again how this casting process can successfully work for any director.

I have divided the entire casting process into 6 sessions:

> Part A. Mandatory Casting Sessions
> 1. The Audition (Deciding Who Is NOT Right)
> 2. The First Callback (Watching Actor Chemistry)
> 3. The Second Callback (Deciding Who IS Right)
>
> Part B. Optional Casting Interviews and Tests
> 4. Checking References (Who Has Worked With Them)
> 5. Actor Interviews (Getting to Know Them)
> 6. Screen Tests (When in Doubt)

I believe this 6-step process is one of the best ways to cast actors. Most directors will find their cast after the first 3 steps, but if you still cannot decide on your actors after the last callback, the next three steps are good ways to help you make the final casting choices.

But no matter how many steps of this process you use, it's vitally important that you personally direct your first audition and all the callbacks using the main *casting strategy* I discuss in Chapter 14: *The Top Three Qualities Directors Look For in Casting*!

Note: If for any reason you cannot direct these auditions or callbacks yourself, ask the casting director (or producer) to follow this process as closely as possible.

Part A. Mandatory Casting Sessions

1. The Audition (Deciding Who Is NOT Right)

I never try to cast an actor from the first audition. For me, the first audition is about discovering which actors are *not right* for any of the roles. I know this may sound strange, but for most professional directors, the callbacks are where we make our final actor choices. (So please make sure your producer has budgeted for at least one callback session!)

It's also important to understand that during all the casting sessions, the *director* (you) needs to control the room. The casting director and producers are there to support you and give you their ideas on the roles, but you should be the one that decides how you want to run each casting session.

When you first start directing, this will be hard. Experienced casting directors (and producers) have fixed casting procedures of their own. But as you get more experience, you can work with the casting director to organize the casting sessions the way you'd like.

1. Depending on the size and budget of the film, the people that attend the first casting session are the director, producer, casting director, reader, and cameraperson.

2. Make sure the actors are scheduled *not less* than 10 minutes apart. Casting sessions usually run over time, so depending on how many pages the actors are reading as well as your personal casting style, 10 minutes for each actor should be enough time for the first session.

3. When the actor enters the room, introduce yourself first (remember *trust*), then the producer, casting director, and reader. It's your choice if you want to introduce anyone else.

4. The actor then records the camera slate with their full name, the role they are reading for, the agency representing them, and any other information you or your casting director require.

5. Next, show them the area of the room where they can *freely move around*. Make sure they know the camera will follow them so they won't be restricted if they feel like moving during their reading.

6. You then ask the actor if they have any questions. Most actors will have no questions, but if they do it's usually about their character, a story point clarification, or the correct pronunciation of a certain word. Whatever the questions are, answer them simply and quickly.

7. An important part of this first audition process is to *NOT* give any direction to the actor until *after* they have finished their first reading. There are several reasons for this.

    First, if an actor shows you what they have prepared on their first reading (without any direction from you), you get to see their own version of the character. Second, you see how prepared the actor is before you give them an adjustment for the second reading. Third, you have another great way to establish trust between actor and director.

8. The chair! Many actors have been trained to sit down when they read their lines for an audition. Well I'm sorry, but unless the character is confined to a bed or wheelchair, I believe actors should be standing up when they do their lines. Sitting affects their breathing and posture, and restricts their bodily movement.

    So what do you do when an actor asks if they can sit in a chair? You say "of course" because you don't want to change anything they have prepared for their first reading. But on the second reading, take the chair away so you can see them read standing up.

9. The camera starts and you call "action" for the first take.

10. When the actor has finished, thank them for a good first read and tell them you're going to give them an *adjustment* (a change of objective) for the second take. (I cover this in more detail in Chapter 14.)

11. The camera starts and you call "action" for the second take.

12. When the actor has finished, thank them for coming in and tell them the casting director (or producer) will contact them if there is a callback. When the actor leaves the room the director, casting director, and producer quickly make their casting notes on that particular actor.

13. The next actor is brought in, and the whole process repeats.

14. At the end of this first casting session, the director, casting director, and producer compare notes and decide on a *short list* of actors to

bring back to the first callback session. Depending on how many actors have read for each role, you will usually want 3–5 actors to come back for each role in your first callback session.

Remember, the first audition is primarily about deciding who will *not* be coming to the callbacks, so the rule here is "when in doubt, bring them to the callback."

15. Reviewing, evaluating, and critiquing audition performance (See Chapter 14: *20 Qualities Directors Look For in Actors*).

Most importantly, remember to "*cast for acting ability first and look second.*" Unless an actor needs to have a very specific look for a role (i.e., Peter Dinklage in *Game of Thrones*), your priority is to cast actors who give you the most consistent and believable readings in *ALL* your auditions and callbacks.

Remember, an actor's physical look for a specific character can usually be successfully enhanced, altered, or even changed through the magic of makeup, hair, and wardrobe (Charlize Theron in *Monster*) or through computerized visual effects (Andy Serkis as Gollum in *Lord of the Rings*).

Note: If an actor is chosen because they have the perfect look for a role, but their acting ability and performance skills are limited, your job as a director is going to be very, very difficult — especially when the producer taps you on the shoulder after a take and says, "Make them better!"

2. The First Callback (Watching Actor Chemistry)

Callbacks are different from an audition. It's here that you pair up the actors to watch the *chemistry* between them. For this first callback, you will want to spend more time with the actors; budget about 15 minutes per session.

Also, all the actors should show up at the same time (if possible) so you can mix and match them as you see fit. If applicable, choose a different scene for them to read than the one from their first audition.

Before any callback, make a list of the actors you want to read together and give it to the casting director as soon as possible. Depending on their personal schedules, the first actors you would like to read for you should be the ones you are most interested in. If they work out, those first readings will be the "standard" you gauge the other actors' performances by.

1. Depending on the size and budget of the film, the people who attend the first callback session are the director, producer, casting director, and cameraperson. (There is no reader.)

2. Tell the casting director the order you would like to see each grouping of two actors.

3-13. (Follow the same procedure as the first audition.)

14. At the end of the first callback session, the director, casting director, and producer compare notes and decide on a short list of actors to bring back to the second callback session. For this last session, you will want the top two actor choices for each role to come back.

15. (Reviewing, evaluating, and critiquing the first callback performance is the same as the audition.)

Tip: Start thinking about the *blocking* of a scene during your casting callback sessions by experimenting with the actors during their callbacks.

3. The Second Callback (Deciding Who IS Right)

At this final callback, you now have two actors competing for each role. Have all the actors show up at the same time; if possible, choose a new scene for them to perform together. You should budget about 20 minutes per session.

1-13. (Follow the same procedure as the first audition.)

14. At the end of this second callback session, the director, casting director, and producer compare notes and decide on the final cast of the film. The casting director or producer sends out an offer to each actor's agent, and the negotiations, waiting games, and film-schedule changes begin!

15. (Reviewing, evaluating, and critiquing the second callback performance is the same as the first callback.)

Note: Depending on how these two callback sessions have gone, you may want to schedule several more to "fine-tune" your actor choices. Again, this will depend on the time you have and the budget of your film, as well as how much experience you have as a director.

Part B. Optional Casting Interviews and Tests

The next three parts of the casting process are optional. Most directors who follow the first three parts of this casting process will never use these options. By the time they complete the second callback, they have had enough opportunity to view and choose the best actors for their film.

However, if you still can't decide between two actors for a role, OR you are working on a big-budget movie and have the time, OR you are working for a studio or network who insist on screen tests and interviews, OR you are working with a major star who is already part of the picture deal and has approval on the other lead actors, these last three options will help you and your producer finally execute your most critical casting choices.

4. Checking References (Who Has Worked With Them)

Checking actor references is something you can probably do on your own. Screen some of their previous films, and get the names of the directors who worked with them. If you can, contact these directors and talk to them about their experiences (good and bad) working with the actor. It's always interesting to hear what another director has to say about an actor after they have worked with them on the set for a few weeks or a few months.

5. Actor Interviews (Getting to Know Them)

Informal interviews, such as going for coffee or dinner, are a great way to get to know the actor personally and also help create trust between the actor and the director.

Many times the choice of an actor comes down to how the director and the actor can get along personally — especially if the role is very emotional and dramatic and/or the shooting schedule is long and demanding. (And don't forget, during this meeting the actor is also "interviewing" you!)

6. Screen Tests (When in Doubt)

There are basically two versions of a screen test. The first screen test is a "filmed first audition" by an actor if they are not available to come to your casting session because of prior commitments.

In these cases, the actors are sent the sides (the scene pages you want them to read) as well as *exact instructions* on the adjustment you want them to make after their first reading. The actors usually get a friend or colleague to run the camera and also be the reader.

The video quality of these filmed auditions is usually not very good (it may have been shot with a cellphone camera in a hotel room at night), but you should get a good idea of the actor's physicality and their performance based on the adjustment you gave them. If this filmed audition works out, then arrangements are made for the actor to have a live audition with the director.

The second kind of screen test is one that is professionally shot by a film crew and the director after the casting sessions are completed. The actors who are asked to do this kind of screen test are usually auditioning for a major role on a movie or as a lead character in a TV series.

These "management" screen tests are viewed by the director, producers, and studio executives so they can get a good look at the actor's performance as well as what he or she physically looks like on film.

14

DIRECTING ACTORS IN CASTING

Directors often fall into a "dream lover" approach to casting. This means having an idea/ideal of the character in your head and searching for the actor who matches it. This gets you into a lot of trouble. —JUDITH WESTON*

WHY AUDITIONS ARE THE "BOTTLENECK" OF THE FILM INDUSTRY

The casting session (audition) can be an intimidating experience for both actors and directors alike because it's the place where "both sides of the table" have only a few minutes to make bold, creative choices. Choices that could affect ALL of our careers!

For actors it takes a lot of guts to walk into a small, windowless room and have 10 minutes to "show their stuff" in front of complete strangers. But it's just as tough for directors as well! How can we correctly decide, in less than 10 minutes, who is right for a particular role?

Once you start casting, you realize that a big part of the success (or failure) of your film rests on the final choice of actor for a specific character in your story.

Directors must quickly judge an actor's personal qualities and professional skills and determine if they are right for a role. Even more challenging, the final decision to cast an actor is almost never left up to the director alone.

Producers, network/studio executives, casting directors, and even the dentist bankrolling your indie film may all want a say on who is right for a particular lead role.

Directing Actors: Creating Memorable Performances for Film & Television (Michael Wiese Productions, 1996)

During your initial producer concept meetings, you may have all agreed on the specific type and look of a character, but when an actor enters the room and gives you an authentic and moving performance that deviates from your original concept, a casting "bottleneck" emerges.

CASTING ACTORS BASED ON SUBCONSCIOUS EMOTIONAL PERCEPTIONS

A good audition means we believe the actor as the character. But what does the word "believe" actually mean? After an audition, the director might choose one actor for a role, but the producer will pick someone else. Or vice-versa. So who is right? Well, from each of their perspectives, they both are!

In an audition, everyone looks for different traits or qualities in an actor based on their own professional experiences, creative tastes, and personal *emotional triggers*! Some of these triggers are conscious. and some are unconscious; choosing actors (like any other creative choice) is an emotional and subjective response.

As I discussed in Chapter 5, our physiological needs tend to influence our perceptions of others, and the way we make sense of the world around us has a direct influence on *how* we perceive and interact with others.

This means other people's reactions matter greatly to us, and these reactions have a huge influence on how we act toward others. So if you are in a casting session, part of your decision on who you like for a role will be partially based on your *subconscious* personal and emotional perceptions.

TOP 3 QUALITIES DIRECTORS LOOK FOR IN CASTING

During the casting process, directors look for a variety of character traits and qualities in every actor. The most important qualities are acting ability, physical characteristics, and chemistry with other actors.

Because there is never enough time to work with actors in a casting session, along with the added pressure of producers and others also making casting decisions, here are the top three qualities you should concentrate on when casting actors:

1. Do they look the part?

Many actors could be cast in a role just by entering the room! He (or she) doesn't have to say anything — they just LOOK like the character so much that they ARE the character!

"Looking the part" is a big plus for short films or TV series when you don't have a lot of time to build secondary characters, so an actor really resembling the character you had envisioned is a good *first step* in making them believable to your audience.

But be careful! Having an actor who looks like a character is only part of the casting process. Finding out if they can "act believably" is the bigger and more important part — something you find out next.

2. Can they take direction?

Experienced actors will make a choice when they enter the casting room. They will have decided on who their character is (based on the written scene and the character description) and will then give us *their interpretation*. But many times this is not the exactly the characterization we had in mind, so what you do now is give the actor some "direction" by asking for an *adjustment*.

An adjustment is when you have the actor play the same scene again, but this time you give them a *different objective* for the second take. This adjustment gives the director a good idea if the actor can take direction AND if they have range. (You really want to find these out before you are on set!)

Changing the actor's scene objective means giving them a new "goal or want" for the scene, then having the actor play that objective. If you need to do another take, you can either have the actor up the stakes of that objective (go from "demand" to "threaten") or give them a totally new objective change.

3. Do they have performance range?

This is basically saying, "Can they act?" and you usually discover this after you give the actor a good scene-objective adjustment. Did the actor play the objective change believably? Were they believable in a tense, dramatic scene? Were they believable in a fast-paced comedy? Do they understand the subtext of the scene? Were they "in the moment" during the scene?

When it comes to judging an actor's performance in your film, many producers and executives use this rule: If the acting is good — it's the actors. If the acting is bad — it's the director's fault. (Who said this business was fair?)

LOOKING FOR "MAGIC PERFORMANCE MOMENTS"

Like any art form, there are very few rules or guidelines in filmmaking (but lots of opinions), and every director has an opinion on how to cast actors. And one of my very "strong opinions" is that *you don't always have to give actors an objective adjustment that relates to the scene they are reading!*

Since my goal for the first audition is to find out who is NOT right for a part, after the actor's first reading I give them a change of objective that is the *opposite* of the one they just played. What I'm looking for here is a quick way to find out if the actor is listening to me, if they have range in their performance, and if they can take direction.

I call this technique *"looking for magic moments"* because the objective change I give them *may not be relevant* to all the text in the scene — but if you know what to look for, you will discover "magic performance moments" within the scene where the actor has taken your notes and made them work.

For example: If the written scene describes the character as extremely angry, and the writer has the character yelling at their partner, the actor's first read will most likely have them yelling (loudly and angrily) at their partner. Why? Because that is what the script text says, and actors understand that the "written moment" is what you are probably looking for!

So for the adjustment change, I give them an *opposite objective* (or opposite action verb) such as: "Let's do it again, but this time I would like you *to flirt with her."* This adjustment may have nothing to do with the written scene, but if the actor is well trained and they've listened to me, they'll take that note and create a very real and believable performance — but only within certain moments of the written text.

This effective technique will not only show you if the actor listened to you and took your direction, but will also reveal their performance range.

20 QUALITIES DIRECTORS LOOK FOR IN ACTORS

Whether you review the auditions from your notes or by looking at video, the following checklist contains 20 general traits and qualities you will want to look for in any actor. However, you will also need to add to this list the specific qualities and traits of the individual characters in your film before deciding on whom to cast.

1. Assessing the performance. (Look at both the actor's physical characteristics and their acting abilities.)
2. Typecasting vs. performance casting. (Think outside the box when it comes to actors portraying characters.)
3. Character relationships. (Which actors could play well together? Does the chemistry work?)
4. Make a note of all the negative qualities. (This could be from the actor's physical characteristics or performance issues.)
5. Remember that motivation always determines behavior, and also shapes the character. (What our needs are will decide what actions we take.)
6. Is the character type in the actor? (Does the actor physically look like the character? Do they have personal mannerisms and quirks that will work for the character?)
7. What is the persona/image of the character? (In the script, what does the writer say about the character's physical and emotional traits?)
8. What is the persona/image of the actor? (What does the actor think of himself? What personal qualities does he exhibit?)
9. What is the actor's rhythm and movement pattern? (How does the actor walk? How does he sit? How does he stand?)
10. Do they incorporate changes quickly? (These can be anything from beat changes to unexpected events.)
11. Was the adjustment (change of direction) believable? (Judge the strengths and weaknesses of the actor from your objective adjustment.)

12. How well did they listen? (Are they focused? Can they play in the moment with another actor?)

13. Did they make active choices? (Are they adept at creating appropriate actions for the character to tell the story rather than just saying the words?)

14. Do they have a clear sense of the character? (Have they done their research? Do they know their "who, what, where, when, and how"?)

15. Can they perform through impulse, not through cues? (Do they react naturally to what is going on around them? Are they good at not anticipating the next line?)

16. Do they react well to problems? (Can they stay in character if another other actor drops their lines? Do they get distracted easily?)

17. Do they know their backstory? (Does the actor know where they have just been, what they are feeling, and where they are going?)

18. Do they know what is important in the scene? (Are they willing to take a "backseat" to an animal, a child, a specific prop, or a visual effect?)

19. Do they understand the character's physical environment? (Are they believable as a prisoner? Is the "fake film set" environment hot or cold?)

20. Do they have a certain charisma about them? (Do heads turn when they enter a room? This is a trait that cannot be taught.)

CHOOSING ACTORS (ACTING ABILITY FIRST — LOOK SECOND)

Before you can make any final decisions on casting, you must know where you stand on the "food chain" of any film you direct. In other words, what are the "office politics"? Are you a first-time director, or are you an award-winning director with 30 years experience? These facts will ultimately determine your relationship (and influence) with actors, producers, studios, and networks.

We have now reached the most decisive and crucial moment in the casting process — the time when everyone involved gets to voice their "opinion" on which actors they want for each role. And unfortunately, this is also the time when the "casting bottleneck" could rear its ugly head.

The most important factor to remember when casting is to choose actors based on *"acting ability first and look second"*! Of course there are always going to be exceptions, but if you start with the premise that you want to cast actors who are believable because they gave the best organic performances (rather than "looking like the character"), you will be better prepared to get the performances you need on set.

Audiences will never know if you wanted a different actor for a role. They only see (on the screen) who you have chosen. And if your story is compelling and the actors are believable, the audience will engage with your film.

As a director, you will find yourself in situations where the "money people" (producers, executives, investors, etc.) love the look of an actor because they "are" the character they have always visualized, and you could be put under pressure to hire that person.

If you agree with their choice (because you also know the actor is a talented performer based on what you've seen during the casting process), then everyone is happy!

But if you are "way down the production food chain," you may have to suck it up and improve your directing skills. There's a chance that an actor who was approved by the "money people" may look the part, but their performance range and acting skills are weak. However, if you disagree with their choices and are high up the "production food chain," then casting actors you want may not be a big issue.

It may seem like I'm picking on the "money people" here, but I'm not. If you are a director and *you* choose an actor just because they look the part (even after the producers wanted someone else who was a better actor), then you will have to live with your choice. And once on set, it's usually too late for anyone to say, "I told you so!"

> Casting sessions are not just to pick actors for a role; they are also a very useful way for a director to improve their script. When you listen to actors performing a scene in the script, you get a real feel for the words and how they flow when different actors read the same scenes. You can actually see (or hear) what works and what doesn't, and it's from the casting sessions that many of your script changes will happen.

15

BLOCKING AND REHEARSING ACTORS ON SET

Cinema is a matter of what's in the frame and what's out.
—MARTIN SCORSESE

NEWTON'S FIRST LAW OF MOTION

In this chapter I'm going to discuss how to efficiently block and rehearse actors on the set, but I first want to mention Sir Isaac Newton's first "Law of Motion." (Don't worry, this isn't going to be a physics lecture. I just want to show how a universal law of physics will help your blocking.)

In the 1687 volume *Philosophiae Naturalis Principia Mathematica*, Sir Isaac Newton states his first Law of Motion: An object at rest tends to stay at rest unless acted upon by an external or unbalanced force, and an object in motion tends to stay in motion with the same speed and in the same direction unless acted upon by an external or unbalanced force.

If we "translate" this Law of Motion into filmmaking terms, we get:

1. "A character who is *stationary* will not move until some *external* physical event or *internal* emotion compels them (or forces them) to move."

2. "A character who is *moving* will not stop until some *external* physical event or *internal* emotion compels them (or forces them) to stop."

In other words, the actor (as the character) must be "physically or emotionally motivated" before they will take any kind of action. *(Motivation Determines Behavior!)*

WHAT IS BLOCKING?

Blocking is essentially the "relationship of the actors to the camera." It is the "physical and emotionally *motivated* movement of the actors relative to the various positions of the camera."

It also helps to think of blocking (or staging) as the choreography of a dance or ballet where all the elements on set (actors, extras, vehicles, crew, equipment, etc.) move in perfect harmony with each other.

When you first start directing, blocking actors can be one of the most frustrating and difficult parts of your job, and if you get it wrong here you could waste valuable shooting time trying to get out of the mess you created! But no matter how experienced you are as a director, before you create your blocking plan and shot list, you need to first complete a detailed analysis of every scene to find the scene objective and the character objectives.

BLOCKING FOR STORY AND CHARACTER

As a film director, your job is to *reveal a character's thoughts or emotions through actions* because actions reveal more about a character than dialogue. Therefore actor movement must have a precise objective and goal. Make sure that every move an actor makes has a *specific purpose.*

To accomplish these objectives, you need to create a personal relationship with each actor so you can work together on every scene to find:

- The emotional structure of the scene (Emotions and feelings)
- The subtext of the scene (What is really going on)
- The physical movement of each character (Blocking or staging)
- The activities of each character (Actor business)
- The pace of the scene (Timing of dialogue and actions)

BLOCKING FOR THE CAMERA

Because *viewer emotion* is the ultimate goal of each scene, camera placement involves knowing which emotion you want the audience to experience at any given moment. So when blocking actors for the camera, you need to drive the blocking emotionally so no actor movement is done aimlessly. You accomplish this by knowing *why* the actor moves; *where* the actor moves; *when* the actor moves; and *how* the actor moves.

1. Two ways to stage space: *across the frame* (left to right & right to left) and *in-depth staging* (foreground to background & background to foreground).

2. When you change the space between characters, you also indicate a change in the relationship.

   If a character walks *toward* another character, that could indicate anger OR happiness. (Any movement toward camera is powerful — the character takes over.) If a character walks *away* from another character, that could indicate fear OR sadness. (Any movement away from camera is weakened — the character's presence is diminished.)

3. Character movement is also a way of expressing opposition and resistance. *Moving* characters create lots of energy — they are dynamic. *Still* characters create less energy — they are peaceful.

4. *The opening position* of each character is a very important element of blocking. Use your story knowledge of a character to imagine their opening position. For example, different character types tend to move to different places in a room. A *strong character* might move to the middle of a room whereas a *weak character* might stay at the side of a room.

5. If you are having trouble deciding how to start a scene, place the actors in their *end positions* and then "reverse engineer" their movements to figure out where they would naturally start the scene.

There is never one interpretation of how a scene should be blocked because every director will block the same scene differently. Blocking actors for the camera is like putting together a complicated picture puzzle — you need to keep moving each piece around until they all fit into place and you can clearly see the whole picture!

> When blocking a scene, experienced directors not only think about their shots, camera positions, and character movement, they also

> consider all the other factors affecting each particular scene: lighting, window placement, vehicle movement, extras, stunts, special effects, time, and budget.

ON-SET PROTOCOL: THE 5 STAGES OF SHOOTING A SCENE

I first learned of the five stages of shooting a scene when I was a 2nd AD on the TV series *The Hitchhiker*. I didn't have a lot of set experience at that time, so when the 1st AD asked me to run the set while he worked on the shooting schedule, I got seriously flustered about the order of how to do things. That's when I heard the dolly grip call my name and quietly say, "Peter, it's *block, light, rehearse, adjust, shoot!*"

These five stages of shooting a scene should be the basic on-set protocol for every filmmaker around the world. However, there are some directors who will not block with the actors first, believing that not doing so will save time. So when the actors arrive on set, the scene is already lit, the camera is in its first position, and the director simply tells the actors where to move to fit the shot. Not good!

Setting up the first shot and lighting the set without blocking the actors first is a disaster waiting to happen, and can create many problems later on: 1) You could end up spending extra time talking to the actors about their blocking before each setup; 2) You might have to adjust your lighting and reframe the camera because the actors move to a different position; 3) You may have to return to a previous camera position because you need to add a shot.

Because the actors don't get a chance to show you their ideas for blocking the scene or get to see what you have planned before you set up the camera, this situation could also seriously undermine your actor/director relationship.

The following five stages of shooting a scene have been proven over and over again to be the most effective methods. If you decide to not fully block a scene, you do so at your own risk by possibly falling behind schedule, dropping shots, and losing the trust of experienced actors.

1. **Blocking** determines where the actors will be on the set, and the location of the first camera position. Always block with the actors before blocking with the camera, and let the actors show you what they want to do first. At this stage, you want to block for actor movement first, not necessarily for performance (how they say their lines). (See below for the more detailed *10-Step Actor/Director Blocking Process.*)

2. **Lighting** is the time when the DOP and the crew light the set and position the camera for the first shot with the second team (stand-ins). The DOP starts with the director's widest shot (or master shot) and gradually ends up with the smallest shot, which requires less lighting and setup time.

3. **Rehearsing** is the full camera rehearsal of the first setup with the actors and the crew. This rehearsal is about the ballet between the camera, sound, and actors, and is mostly technical in nature.

4. **Adjustments (Tweaking/Finals)** are when the DOP and crew make their final technical adjustments to the lights and other equipment based on the changes from the full technical rehearsal. It's also when the hair, makeup, and wardrobe departments do their final "touches" on the actors.

5. **Shooting** is when the camera rolls and you shoot several takes for the first setup. Once you have a "print," you then repeat the process with the second setup until the scene is complete.

Note: When you call "action," your job is to watch both the actors' performances as well as the framing and composition of the camera. Any creative or technical notes you need to give should usually come after the first take (and not during the camera rehearsal). It's only when the camera rolls that the crew and cast give 100%.

THE 10-STEP ACTOR/DIRECTOR BLOCKING PROCESS

The main objective of this 10-step blocking process is to let actors discover their initial movements (blocking) on the set **by themselves first** *with only minimal notes from the director.* This process leads to motivated actor movement and creates more believable performances.

Note: I know this process may seem controversial at first, and many directors will think it's just a waste of time, but the main reasons you allow the actors to block themselves first, without giving detailed direction, are: (1) to discover some new blocking ideas based on what the actors do in the scene; and (2) to increase the "trust factor" in the actor/director relationship by giving directorial notes that organically draw from their blocking.

1. **Running Lines:** The actors get together and "run their lines" (read the scene) before they arrive on set. This is a very important first step when blocking actors. If the actors have been in the previous scene, they will need time to get their heads into the new scene as quickly as possible. Running their lines before bringing them to set ensures they will also be better prepared for the first blocking. If actors are not in the previous scene and are just waiting to come to set, ask them to run their lines for the scene before they show up.

2. **Set Logistics:** Simply show everyone around the set, and point out the various elements they need to know about for this particular scene. Show them the furniture and any doors and windows they may need to use.

   Remember, when actors prepare their scenes they will visualize how they think the set will look based on the scene descriptions and their own imaginations. So when they arrive on a new set, it's going to look different than they imagined. They'll need some time to process this new information before you start blocking.

3. **First Blocking:** You allow the actors to explore the scene by themselves first by showing them where they start. You do not want to give them too much direction now; the objective of this first blocking is to see what the actors have already prepared before you start giving them notes.

4. **First Notes:** Before you block any scene, you must have completed your scene analysis and finalized your blocking plan and list of desired coverage shots. Then, after watching the first blocking, you will be able to adjust the actors more easily based on what they have just shown you and what you require for the scene.

5. **Second Blocking:** The actors go through the scene again, this time incorporating your first blocking notes. It's usually during this

second blocking that the actors and director will get a sense of what the scene is really about and how the actors' movement will appear on screen.

6. **Second Notes:** You give more detailed notes to the actors. By this point in the blocking process, the actors are becoming more comfortable with the staging of the scene and have a better understanding of their character objectives and motivations. You will also be in a better position to move them to specific places on the set for camera positions and lighting.

7. **Third Blocking:** The actors go through the scene for a third time, incorporating the second set of blocking notes from the director.

    Note: This 10-step blocking process is based on blocking a scene at least three times. Based on your budget (shooting time), your experience as a director, and the experience of your actors and crew, you could accomplish this process with two blockings, or you may need four or five — but the blocking process and the end result remain the same.

8. **Blocking for Marks:** The actors run the scene for the DOP so "stop marks" (tape) can be placed on the floor. This is the last part of the blocking process. The actors block the scene again, but pause at the various positions they stopped on set so that tape marks can be put at their feet.

9. **Describe All Shots:** When the actors' positions have been marked, the director, DOP, 1st AD, camera operator, and script supervisor discuss: a) how many setups the director has for the scene; b) the best order to shoot them; and c) what the first setup will be. The actors walk through the scene again ("stops and starts") so the director and DOP can decide on the different camera positions they need to shoot it.

10. **Choose the First Shot:** The first camera setup for the scene (usually the widest shot or the master shot) is chosen by the DOP with the actors still present. (The DOP will always know the quickest and most efficient way of shooting any scene, so it's in the director's best interest to let the DOP choose the shooting order. The majority of time spent on a set is used for lighting and camera placement.)

Tip: In television speed is essential, so try and block some scenes so that your action takes place *in one direction* to avoid turning the camera around for reverses.

SCENE TRANSITIONS (LAST SHOT/FIRST SHOT BLOCKING SYSTEM)

If you are nervous or uncomfortable blocking and directing actors because you lack on-set experience, this section on scene transitions will show you a simple strategy you can use to help your blocking.

As I mentioned earlier, to fully understand how to block any scene you must first know the scene objectives and each character's textual and subtextual objectives. However, you should also know the following four scene transitions, which are the shots you want to cut together, one after another.

Let's say you are figuring out how to camera-block Scene 22.

The first fact you need to know is when (and where) the characters were *LAST SEEN*. (Was it in the scene before? Was it ten scenes earlier? Have the characters ever been seen before?) Knowing these answers will determine how each character could enter this scene. (Backstory.)

1. What is the *LAST* shot of the previous scene? (Let's assume the last shot of Scene 21 is a wide shot of an apartment building. Now what do you think would make a good scene transition to the first shot of Scene 22?)

2. What is the *FIRST* shot of the scene you are blocking? (Let's assume the first shot of Scene 22 is a close-up of a doorknob turning and the door slowly opening.)

3. What is the *LAST* shot of the scene you are blocking? (Let's assume the last shot of Scene 22 is a medium shot of your actor walking up to a window and looking out.)

4. What is the *FIRST* shot of the next scene? (Let's assume the first shot of Scene 23 is an exterior wide shot of the actor from Scene 22 looking out a window. The camera then cranes down to reveal a medium shot of another actor sitting in a car watching the actor in the window.)

Once you have these answers, your DOP and camera operator will be able to watch the blocking and make suggestions regarding where the camera should go to cover the scene. And because you have figured out all your scene transitions, you know where and how you want to start and end each scene so they all cut together perfectly!

10 QUESTIONS TO ASK BEFORE BLOCKING A SCENE

1. Do I understand the writer's intentions? (Plot and themes)
2. What is the objective of this scene? (What is the scene intention?)
3. What is each character's scene objective? (What do they want?)
4. What normal activities would the characters be doing? (Actor business)
5. What are the characters' emotional states? (What are their story arcs?)
6. Where is the focus of interest at each moment? (The main emphasis)
7. What is more important: business or dialogue? (What to focus on)
8. How do I want the audience to react? (Tension? Laughter?)
9. How much time should I allow to shoot this scene? (The schedule)
10. What kind of coverage do I need? (Result of above answers)

16

DIRECTING THE CAMERA

*I'm a storyteller — that's the chief function of
a director. And they're moving pictures, let's
make 'em move! —* **HOWARD HAWKS**

THE DIRECTOR/DOP RELATIONSHIP

The director and director of photography (DOP) relationship is one of the most important collaborative partnerships on any film set. Not only does a director need a DOP who has all the visual and technical skills to make a film "look great," the smart director also wants a DOP who has the creative sensibility to understand the subtext of the story and the subtle nuances of an actor's performance.

The director of photography is responsible for the overall photographic look of a film, collaborating closely with the production designer to create the specific look and tone of the film based on the director's visual concept.

The DOP designs the lighting for each scene and works with the director to choose the proper lenses and specific camera movements for each shot that help to visually tell the story.

Every director and DOP relationship is unique because they each have their own professional experiences, artistic sensibilities, and personal insecurities. Throw into this mix the high stress and tension of a film set, and you could have a recipe for disaster if this team is not a good fit!

THE LANGUAGE OF THE CAMERA

One of the best expressions I've heard describing the filmmaker's main tool for making movies is *the camera is the director's paintbrush*. Today, film and digital cameras come in all shapes, sizes, and formats. As a director, you need to know and understand the various camera techniques that can enhance the visual story-telling power of your film.

This knowledge is crucial because the more correctly you can communicate a technical detail to the DOP and the crew, the better chance you have of getting it!

The following reference guide is a list of basic camera techniques you should know. Every director and DOP will have a slightly different version of the following examples, but you can't go wrong using this guide.

Shot Size (example: a person)
ECU — Extreme Close-Up (the eye)
TCU — Tight Close-Up (forehead to chin)
CU — Close-Up (top of head to just below the chin)
MCU — Medium Close-Up (below the throat to just above the head)
MS — Medium Shot (the body from the waist up)
FS — Full Shot (full figure of subject from head to toe)
WS — Wide Shot (subject shown in relationship to their surroundings)
LS — Long Shot (subject shown in a smaller scale to their surroundings)
ELS — Extreme Long Shot (camera is a great distance from the subject)
OSS — Over Shoulder Shot (over shoulder of person A to see person B)
POV — Point of View (shot from another person's perspective)

Camera Lenses (based on 35 mm format)
Wide-angle lenses are lenses with *short focal lengths* (18 mm to 35 mm) that make spatial distances greater. They create deep focus where both the foreground and background images are sharp. (*Citizen Kane*)

Standard lenses are lenses with a *normal focal length* range (35 mm to 55 mm) that create an angle of view that appears "natural" to a human eye.

Long/telephoto lenses are lenses with *long focal lengths* (70 mm to 300 mm) that compress distant objects and bring them closer. They create short focus in a frame where the foreground is in focus and the background is out of focus.

Zoom lenses are lenses that have *variable focal lengths* and can be used to quickly change a shot from wide angle to normal to telephoto. "Zooming" means you actually "zoom in or out" on a subject while the camera is rolling. One example of a zoom lens designed for 35 mm cameras is the "10:1," which has a variable focal length of 25 mm–250 mm.

Macro lenses are specialized lenses with a very *narrow depth of field* used for extreme "macro" close ups. They come in focal lengths ranging from 50 mm to 200 mm.

Fisheye lenses are specialized *super wide-angle lenses* (7 mm to 16 mm) that create a distorted view of the subject.

Depth of Field

The *focal length* of a lens (wide angle to telephoto) affects the depth of field of a shot by how much the background, middle ground, and foreground are in focus.

Camera Angles

Straight Angle: The camera is placed at the *normal eye level* of a subject and is the most common camera angle in film. (Used to make the audience identify more easily with a character or feel equal to a character.)

Low Angle: The camera *looks up* at a character or object. (Used to show fear, respect, authority.)

High Angle: The camera *looks down* on a character or object. (Used to show vulnerability, inferiority, weakness.)

Bird's-Eye Angle: The camera is placed in an unnatural and extreme position *high and directly overhead* a subject. (Used to show insignificance, godlike power, or extreme exaltation.) (*The Shawshank Redemption*)

Dutch Angle: The camera is *tilted* on an angle at a character or object. (Used to show tension, altered states, instability.)

Camera Movement

Pan Shot: A horizontal movement of a camera. (Left to right or right to left.)

Tilt Shot: A vertical movement of a camera. (Up and down.)

Crane Shot: The camera is mounted on a large, wheeled crane. Some cranes have seats for an operator and a focus puller. Other cranes just have the camera mounted on one end and remote-control camera operations on the other. (Creates big up-down and/or in-out sweeping movements.)

Jib Arm: The camera is mounted on one end of a small metal boom with the camera controls and a counterweight at the opposite end. The jib arm itself is usually mounted on a tripod or on a dolly. (Moves the camera in a sweeping, arc-like motion vertically and horizontally at the same time.)

Handheld Shot: The camera is held by the operator as they walk or run with the action. (Creates a shaky or jerky camera effect.)

Steadicam Shot: The camera is mounted on a specially designed stabilizing arm. (Creates a smooth or gliding camera effect.)

Dolly Shot (Tracking Shot): Camera is placed on a wheeled platform with rails. The dolly shot *does change* the visual perspective of the frame (the way objects appear to the eye).

Zoom Shot: The use of a zoom lens to move closer or farther away from a subject. The zoom *does not change* the visual perspective of the frame (the way objects appear to the eye).

Dolly-In/Zoom-Out Shot: Used to keep a foreground object stationary while the background moves away from the object.

Dolly-Out/Zoom-In Shot: Used to keep a foreground object stationary while the background moves toward the object.

Pedestal: The camera is mounted on a fixed column or pedestal, usually on a dolly. (Moves vertically up or down.)

Camera Slider: The camera is attached to a movable metal track that can be attached to a tripod or dolly. (Moves the camera a few feet left or right to get more camera-angle options during a shot.)

Aerial Shot: The camera is mounted on a helicopter or in a small plane and is used mostly for wide establishing shots of settings such as a city, mountains, prairies, or oceans, etc.

Drone Shot: A drone is a small, unmanned aircraft mounted with a remote-control camera. Drone camera shots are used to photograph locations that are impossible for a film crew to shoot or for aerial shots that a helicopter or small plane cannot physically or safely get to.

Rack Focus: This is an "in-camera" movement that changes the focus from one subject to another while the camera is rolling. (Used with longer lenses that have less depth of field.)

THE PSYCHOLOGY OF THE CAMERA

The "psychology of the camera" refers to the *visual meanings* of a particular shot or camera angle. Where you put the camera, what lens you use, and your framing choices increase the audience's understanding of what the scene is really about and what the characters are feeling.

Audiences will assume that every shot or word of dialogue in a film is there to further the story. Therefore each shot you use should contribute to the story and the theme you are trying to convey. So when you are planning your shots, ask yourself: "What do I want the audience to *see, hear, and feel* at this particular moment?"

Here are six basic "camera options" a director can use to help heighten viewer understanding (text) and emotion (subtext) of a story:

Lens

The lens is a powerful storytelling tool. Lenses expand or compress space, so when you choose a lens you are also choosing the "visual space" a shot takes place in. Before you choose a lens for a shot, ask yourself: "How *intimate* do I want to be with the character, and *how* do I represent that visually?"

Depth

The *illusion* of depth is a big part of visual storytelling. To achieve this "illusion" of depth in a two-dimensional medium, you need to block your scenes with an eye for depth by composing your shots within these three distinct depth planes: foreground, midground, and background.

Focus

One of the main jobs of a director is to direct the attention of the audience to certain areas within the frame. So when you are composing a shot, *where* you place the focus is determined primarily by what is important in the "plot story" or the "thematic story" at that particular time.

Frame

Visual composition should make an emotional statement to the audience, so the meaning, emotion, and framing of each shot needs to come from detailed script analysis. Before framing any shot, ask: "What is the *story objective* of the scene? What do I want the audience to *know* about this scene?"

Angle

The distance the camera is from a character affects the identification of the character with the audience. Here are three "angles of view" for the camera:

Objective: The audience point of view. The camera is placed outside (away from) the action. Example: A wide shot of any action.

Subjective: The camera acts as the viewer's eyes. The camera is placed inside (close to) the action. Example: A medium shot of a person.

Point of View: What the character is seeing. The camera is the action. Example: Characters looking directly into the lens.

Motion

We don't call a film a "motion picture" (or "moving pictures" or "movies") for nothing. In the truest sense of the word, "motion" is about *camera movement*. It's about moving the camera in some way that progresses the audience's understanding of the story — as well as keeps the scene visually interesting.

So as you design your blocking plan and create your shot list, ask yourself: Why do I want the camera to move here? Is it to follow a specific action, reveal an important piece of information, or to reposition the camera for a better frame?

Motion also applies to *screen direction*, which helps viewer orientation. For example, every world map is drawn with north at the top and south at the bottom, so if a character is traveling from Los Angeles to New York their "visual" onscreen travel will be from left to right.

THE 180-DEGREE RULE AND CROSSING THE LINE

Line of Axis: Before blocking any scene, you should know how the *180-degree rule* will affect your choice of camera positions and the movement of your characters. Understanding this rule needs to start early in prep when you begin creating your shot lists and storyboards.

The "180-degree rule" states that if you are filming a scene with two characters (a "2 shot"), there is an "invisible line" between them. The camera should always stay *on one side of that line* (within the 180 degrees) to keep proper screen direction. In most cases, this "line of axis" is determined by where all the actors are positioned (and which way they are looking) in the master shot or your widest shot.

For example, if you are shooting a 2 shot of Meghan *looking camera right* at Andrew (and Andrew *looking camera left* at Meghan), Meghan still needs to be *looking camera right* at Andrew when you move the camera for her CU — and vice-versa.

Jump Cut: Placing your camera on the other side of the line when doing coverage is called "crossing the line" and will result in an editing *jump cut* because the two characters who are talking to each other will now look like they're not talking to each other when the scene is cut together.

COMPOSITION, DEPTH, AND THE RULE OF THIRDS

The "human eye" watches a movie based on several factors (movement, color, leading lines, points of focus), and the art of "pointing audience attention" to a specific place in the frame is achieved through *composition*.

Composition refers to how all the cinematic elements within a frame are arranged and balanced. EVERYTHING in a frame is important. Good composition shows not only the relationship between the characters, but between the characters and all the other elements in the frame as well.

To direct the audience to the central story points in a scene, a shot is composed using the *rule of thirds*, wherein the frame is divided both horizontally and vertically into nine imaginary sections. These sections create reference points that act as guides for composing frames that range from pleasing to unpleasant, depending on the director's vision.

Because film is a two-dimensional medium, when thinking of composition you also want to *compose for depth*. A frame with depth is always more dynamic than a flat frame, so by finding creative ways to add the *illusion of depth* to your frame, you create a more natural three-dimensional feeling.

FINDING YOUR KEY FRAMES

Key frames in filmmaking are a sequence of drawings that show important "moments" in the story. Key frames differ from a storyboard in that a storyboard usually shows the various shots the director wants to shoot in a scene, but one storyboard panel (shot) could contain several key frames of a story moment or action.

To find the key frames in a scene, start with your first "key story moment image" and then think about what other specific images (or "frames") you need to connect in that scene to tell the story. Keep in mind that one shot (i.e., a long dolly shot) could include a single key frame or multiple key frames.

BLOCKING CAMERA CHOICES

Your camera choices can either enhance or detract the audience's understanding of what is happening in the scene, so *where* you put the camera (shots and angles) is determined by asking:

- What is the scene about? (scene objective)
- What is important in the scene? (dialogue, action)
- What do the characters want? (character objectives)
- What emotions do you want the audience to experience? (feelings)
- Whose POV is being expressed? (the writer, the character, the director)
- What distance are you from the subject? (size of the shot)
- What is your relationship to the subject? (choice of lenses)

The *dramatic circle of action* (where you eventually put the camera) is determined by the size of the area you want to shoot.

- You can place the camera *outside* the action to keep some distance from the action. (Example: Wide shot of a football game.)
- You can place the camera *inside* the action so the action moves around the camera. (Example: Handheld close-ups of two actors fighting.)

Reasons to Move the Camera
- Move for emphasis. (The camera moves into an actor)
- Move to emphasize a character in a group. (Pan or dolly)
- Transfer attention from one character to another. (Pan, dolly, or focus)
- To connect movement from one space to another. (Pan from a door to a desk, or Steadicam from one room to another)

Static or Moving
- Static camera (Subjects can be still or moving)
- Static subjects (Camera can be still or moving)
- Moving camera (Subjects can be still or moving)
- Moving subjects (Camera can be still or moving)

Subjective and Objective Camera Angles
- A *subjective* camera angle is a shot taken close to the 180 line. (You can see the face and eyes more clearly.)
- An *objective* camera angle is a shot taken perpendicular to the 180 line. (It is wider — more profile to the actor.)

Camera height is used to show physical (or status) relationships between people. In real life, there are two kinds of *status* relationships:
- Equal to equal (Good cop & bad guy/doctor & doctor)
- Superior to inferior (Judge & defendant/teacher & student)

DIRECTING THE POSTPRODUCTION

Editing is where movies are made or broken.
Many a film has been saved and many a film has been
ruined in the editing room. —JOE DANTE

3 STAGES OF "WRITING" THE FINAL SCRIPT

When a script is first written, the writer goes through a series of first drafts before it gets financed and is ready for preproduction. Once the script gets into the hands of the director, crew, and actors, it will go through three more critical stages of rewrites, modifications, and revisions.

Stage 1 (Preproduction): The script is modified during preproduction with notes from the director, producers, and studio/network executives for creative, technical, or logistical reasons. Once actors have been cast, more changes will occur during the script read-through and actor rehearsals.

Stage 2 (Production): The script (mostly dialogue) is again altered when the director and actors block and shoot each scene.

Stage 3 (Postproduction): The script (story) is again modified (and scenes sometimes rearranged) when the editor and director assemble all the scenes to "visually tell their version of a compelling story with believable characters."

It is in this last editing stage that the movie finally comes together. It's the critical job of the director to keep track of what the story is (really) about through all three stages.

THE DIRECTOR/EDITOR RELATIONSHIP

Who you choose as your editor will have a big impact on the final success of your film. So what qualities should a director look for in an editor? You want an experienced editor who understands your creative style and your personal sensibility. You want an editor who can be objective and speak their mind. You want an editor who understands the new technologies and can handle the numerous technical aspects of postproduction. In short, you want an editor who is a creative partner and not just a "cutter."

THE DIRECTOR'S ROLE IN POSTPRODUCTION

Every film goes through different postproduction stages based on the complexity of the story elements (action, visual effects) and how much editing time (budget) was scheduled, so the following list is an overview of the director's role during postproduction on most films.

> It's hard to imagine all the new technologies (faster computers, advanced editing software, 8K-?K, 3D, virtual reality) that will happen in the next few years and how they will impact the creative, logistical, and financial quality of the production and postproduction stages of any film. With that in mind, I have not included any specific 35 mm film postproduction stages on this list since almost every "film" produced today is being shot on a digital format.

1. Viewing Dailies

The director looks at all the good ("printed") takes from each shooting day with the editor and chooses the best ones so the editor can begin the picture assembly. Directors can choose to view dailies at the end of each shooting day (since digital footage can be viewed immediately), or they can wait until the end of production to view all the dailies at once.

The advantage of viewing dailies during production is that you get to see how the visual style of the film is progressing. You can check the technical aspects of the shoot (focus, camera movement, lighting, sound), evaluate actor performances, and make adjustments before the next day's shooting.

When watching dailies, be as objective a possible so you get a real sense of what is working and what is not. As you make your comments, the editor will take detailed notes for later reference as they begin the rough assembly of your film.

Watching dailies is an important process for the director, and your *first reactions* to the dailies (good or bad) are critical because you will quickly lose your objectivity after viewing these takes over and over again during the editing stage.

2. Picture Assembly

This is the scene-by-scene assembly (based on the shooting-script scene order) of all the best takes the director picked after watching the dailies. The picture assembly shows the director and producer the basic story flow, and also gives them an idea of the length of the film based on the script supervisor's timing of the shooting script.

Editor and director preferences vary here depending on whether they want to use just master shots for the scene assembly or both master shots and basic coverage.

3. Rough Cuts

After the director has viewed the picture assembly and made notes, the editor creates a first rough cut of the film using the master shots and coverage they feel works best. Depending on the director/editor relationship, some directors will sit with the editor as they create the rough cut and make notes as they go. Other directors will leave the editor alone until they finish the rough cut.

I let the editor do the rough cut on their own for two reasons: it gives me a chance to have a rest after shooting, and I want the editor to show me what they think are the "best pieces" of this film. This is why a rough cut is sometimes called the "editor's cut."

Once the rough cut is finished, the director views the film with the producer and editor. This is really the first time the creative team gets to see if the script story structure is working. After the rough cut screening, the director and editor start working scene-by-scene editing the film based on the director's initial vision.

4. Director's Cut

After the director and editor have gone through weeks of editing, and the director is happy with this version, it is called the director's cut. Before this cut is shown to the producers, temporary (temp) music is added, along with any temp voiceovers or temp sound effects that might enhance the viewer's understanding of the story.

If the film has visual effects (which probably won't be ready at this time), the editor will add either simple graphics explaining the visual-effect shot or computer-generated previz (previsualization) shots that give the viewer a better idea of what the final effect will look like.

When the director's cut is finished, the producers screen the cut with the editor and director. This is essentially the first time the producers have seen the director's full version, and the producers now make their notes on the director's cut. The next stage of editing is to create the producer's cut.

5. Producer's Cut
Once the producers have given their notes to the editor and the director, the editor creates another version of the film based on these notes. This version is then screened for the producers and director — and the "creative discussions" begin! (Remember, in filmmaking everyone has an opinion, and this is the producers' opinion on what the final film should look like.)

6. Studio/Network Cut
After the producer's cut has been approved, this version is screened for studio/network executives or private investors. It's at this time that the producers, editor, and director receive more creative notes on the film. The editor and director go back to the editing room to make yet another version of the film.

7. Reshoots and Pickup Shots
Depending on the results of the creative notes from the director, producers, executives, and investors, reshoots and pickups may be scheduled, shot, and inserted into the film. If the director is available, it's always better that he or she directs these reshoots.

8. Test Screenings
Test screenings are a valuable part of the editing process (at any stage) because the creative team gets "fresh eyes" to watch their film and see if the story is working. I've divided these test viewers into four groups:

Civilian viewers who have not read the script and know nothing about your film. These are the most "valuable viewers" (true audience) because they will tell

136

you if the story is working or not. (Did they get confused at certain points? Does the story make sense? Do they believe the characters? What do they think of the actors' performances? How is the technical quality of the film?)

Professional filmmakers who have not read the script and know nothing about your film. These "professional viewers" will tell you if the story is working, but they will also be able to discuss creative and technical details in the cut that "civilian viewers" cannot.

Professional filmmakers who have read the script and also worked on your film. These viewers will give you yet another perspective because they know the material enough to raise certain creative and technical questions.

Relatives and friends: Mothers, fathers, brothers, sisters, boyfriends, girlfriends, husbands, and wives are good for your ego, but they may not be the most unbiased of viewers! ☺

9. Final Cut

This is when the editor and director go through the film frame-by-frame to complete the final edited version of the film based on all the previous creative and technical notes.

From a director's point of view, this part of the editing process can be the most contentious. Very few directors will ever have "right of final cut." By retaining this right, producers and studios get to keep creative control of the product they have paid for.

The directors who are lucky enough to have "final cut approval" of their project are the only ones who can truly call a movie their own. They have the absolute final say on what an audience will see (and won't see) in the story.

10. Fine Cut (Locked Picture)

After all the changes have been reviewed and approved by the person (or persons) who have absolute final-cut approval, the movie will then be considered "locked." This means that no further picture changes can be made — and now the sound designer, music composer, and sound editor can go to work.

11. Sound Design

Before your first day of shooting, you should have an idea of what your soundscape (sounds and music) is going to be. Your sound design is critical. For an audience to totally feel the emotional impact of your film, they need to hear your story world as well as see it. Creative sound design pulls the audience further into the story because good sound makes the images more real.

12. Sound-Spotting Session

Once you have a locked picture, the editor and the sound design team watch the film scene by scene with the director. who discusses the sounds he or she wants to hear at specific moments.

Every movie is filled with many different sounds — from *onscreen* sounds (dialogue, footsteps, vehicles passing by, children laughing in a classroom, rain hitting a window) to *off-screen* sounds (ship horns, train whistles, a radio in another room, airplanes, wind). A good director understands the value of the film's soundscape and will choose specific sounds to enhance scene transitions, dramatic or comedic situations, actor beats, and quiet performance moments.

13. ADR

The ADR session (Automated Dialogue Replacement) is when actors are brought into a sound studio after the picture is locked to replace certain lines of (or add additional) dialogue. ADR is more than just matching a performance or solving a location sound-recording problem. It also gives the director another chance to get a different or even better performance from an actor than the original.

But ADR will not solve all your technical or performance problems. Returning after several months to repeat specific dialogue is difficult even for the most experienced actors because they need to find the same emotional intensity they originally had for each ADR moment.

Remember, some actors have the technical and creative ability to perform good ADR, but many actors do not, so directors need a lot of patience to help actors find those emotional beats and moments again.

14. Voiceovers and Narration

This is when you record voiceover dialogue with actors to clarify certain story moments, or record the film's narration with a specific actor.

15. Music and Songs

Good music has a huge impact on the mood and tone of your film. It can touch your audience on both an emotional and intellectual level by underscoring dramatic moments or giving meaning to thematic images.

Music for your film is created from two sources: *original* music written especially for your film and *prerecorded* music you buy from a sound library. Which one you choose is usually based upon your budget.

If you have budgeted for original music, you want to hire your *music composer* early so you can go over the script and discuss the look and feel of the film, your themes, and your ideas on mood and tone.

During postproduction, let the composer watch a rough cut of the film so he or she can get an idea of the rhythm and pacing of the story as well as your important thematic images. Whether or not you want the composer to hear any temp music is up to you. Some directors do. Some directors don't.

Choosing *songs* for your film follows the same pattern as choosing music. You pay a singer or band to record *original songs* and then you own the rights, or you pay for *preexisting songs* from established artists where you need to obtain the rights. Again, which one you choose is usually dependent upon the budget of your film.

Whether you choose original or prerecorded music, film music serves two functions: as underscore and as source music. *Underscore* music adds another creative layer to a film by enhancing dramatic moments or musically commenting on a specific scene beat. *Source* music comes from "a source within the scene" such as a song on a radio or a character playing the piano.

16. Music-Spotting Session

If you have the budget for original music, the director shows the composer the locked picture cut. Just like the sound-spotting session, you watch the film scene-by-scene with the composer, discussing what music cues you want at specific moments.

If you don't play music yourself and you don't understand the "music language," just talk to the composer in terms of the emotion you are after in the scene, such as "sad, funny, threatening, foreboding, scary, etc."

By this stage, the composer should have had several meetings with you about the theme and tone of the film. They may even have some thematic music examples you can listen to.

If you don't have the budget for original music, have a spotting session with a music supervisor or producer, who will find you appropriate library music that fits the film's mood and tone.

17. Sound Mix

The sound mix is where all the different sound elements (dialogue, music, and sound effects) are seamlessly blended to create the visceral sound experience you envisioned when you first created your visual concept.

The director's main job during the mix is to make sure all sound levels are correctly balanced. The audience should hear only the sounds or music you want them to. The sound mixers are highly trained professionals, but only you know the subtle sonic and musical nuances you want.

18. Titles and Credits

If the film has a number of visual-effects shots, those images could take weeks or even months after the sound mix to complete. But when ALL the images are finally cut into the film, the titles and credits are created and inserted.

The look of a movie's titles and credits are very important and should not be left to the last minute or created without input from the director and the production designer. The style of your main-title graphics, and how they appear on screen, should be designed to set up the film's tone and mood.

19. Special Visual Effects

The director's role in the creation of visual effects starts early in prep. Designing and creating visual effects is a combination of many talents — director, producers, production designer, DOP, and visual-effects supervisor.

Getting a specific image from your head onto paper, into the 3D computer, and into the finished film is a time-consuming and costly process. Meetings early in prep, collaborations with a storyboard artist, computerized previsualizations, and three-dimensional models are all part of the long process of creating exciting visual effects.

20. Color Correction

One of the last stages of completing a film is color correction, which is not just a technical requirement but also an important story element. This process cannot begin until all visual elements have been completed, approved, and inserted into the final cut.

During production, you may have used different lenses or cameras, lighting will have changed from shot to shot, digital imagery may be overexposed or under-exposed, or your colors and white balances could be off. *Technical color correction* evens out these visual inconsistencies to create images that look consistent both within a scene and throughout the whole film.

Story color correction means enhancing the thematic mood and emotional story points of the film by keeping the color scheme your DOP and production designer have created consistent through every scene.

A FINAL WORD — DIRECTING AUDIENCE EMOTION

According to Walter Murch (an Academy Award–winning film editor/ sound mixer):

> When making a cut, audience emotion is what you should preserve at all costs. The audience will forgive — or not even notice — continuity problems or rhythmic inconsistencies as long as they are engaged by the story.
>
> If you have to give up something in your edit (and you always do), don't ever give up the character emotion or the audience emotion. Remember: each shot (each cut) needs to make a point. Make them laugh or make them cry, but whatever else you do, make the audience care. —WALTER MURCH, *In the Blink of an Eye: A Perspective on Film Editing* (Silman-James Press, 2001)

. . . . AAAAAND CUT!

I always start off my very first Term 1 directing class at the Shanghai Vancouver Film School by telling the new students that we are learning (and speaking) three languages: English, Chinese, and Filmmaking. It is my hope that through this book I have been able to demystify the film-directing process for you by "cracking open the door" and taking you behind the scenes so you can better understand the "*universal* language of filmmaking."

As I said in the introduction to this book, "Directing a movie is actually less complicated than you think. The trick is to learn the 'craft' of filmmaking first and then adapt your personal skills and your creative ability to the 'art' of filmmaking. In other words, there is an 'art and craft' to making movies: you must **learn the craft first — then perfect your art!**"

No matter where you live in the world, we all have our own unique stories to tell. So if you have a compelling story built upon universal themes and you have actors who can make us feel something, then you must direct that film (in your own language) so audiences around the world will be able to observe *your version of the human condition*!

Make the Magic Happen!

Peter

FILMOGRAPHY

Movie References

A Beautiful Mind

The Bourne Identity

Cinderella

Citizen Kane

Django Unchained

Empire of the Sun

Excalibur

Ghostbusters

Gravity

Hell in the Pacific

Jaws

The Karate Kid

Lord of the Rings

Mad Max

The Martian

The Mission

Moneyball

Monster

Monster's Ball

Mr. Smith Goes to Washington

Pearl Harbor

Peter Pan

Philadelphia

Samson and Delilah

The Shawshank Redemption

The Terminator

Titanic

Twister

Whiplash

Television References

Game of Thrones

The Hitchhiker

BIBLIOGRAPHY

Joseph Campbell, *The Hero With a Thousand Faces* (Princeton University Press, 1949)

Joseph Campbell with Bill Moyers, *The Power of Myth* (Anchor Books, 1988)

Kendra Cherry, *The Everything Psychology Book: Explore the Human Psyche and Understand Why We Do the Things We Do* (Adams Media, 2nd edition, 2010)

Harold Clurman, *On Directing* (Free Press, 1972)

Jo-Ellan Dimitrius & Wendy Patrick Mazzarella, *Reading People: How to Understand People and Predict Their Behavior — Anytime, Anyplace* (Ballantine Books, 2008)

Edward Dmytryk, *On Screen Directing* (Focal Press, 1984)

Syd Field, *Screenplay: The Foundations of Screenwriting* (Dell Publishing, 1979)

Uta Hagen with Haskel Frankel, *Respect for Acting* (Macmillan, 1973)

Nicky Hayes, *Understand Psychology: Teach Yourself* (Hodder & Stoughton General Division, 2010)

William Indick, Ph.D., *Psychology for Screenwriters: Building Conflict in Your Script* (Michael Wiese Productions, 2004)

Steven D. Katz, *Shot by Shot: Visualizing from Concept to Screen* (Michael Wiese Productions, 1991)

Tom Kingdon, *Total Directing: Integrating Camera and Performance in Film and Television* (Silman-James Press, 2004)

Abraham Maslow, *Motivation and Personality* (Harper & Row, 1954)

Robert McKee, *Story: Style, Structure, Substance, and the Principles of Screenwriting* (HarperCollins, 1997)

Larry Moss, *The Intent to Live: Achieving Your True Potential as an Actor* (Bantam Books, 2005)

Roberta Marie Munroe, *How Not to Make a Short Film: Secrets from a Sundance Programmer* (Hyperion, 2009)

Walter Murch, *In the Blink of an Eye: A Perspective on Film Editing* (Silman-James Press, 2001)

Nicholas Proferes, *Film Directing Fundamentals: See Your Film Before Shooting* (Focal Press, 2008)

Peter W. Rea and David K. Irving, *Producing and Directing the Short Film and Video* (Focal Press, fifth edition, 2015)

Hester Schell, *Casting Revealed: A Guide for Film Directors* (Michael Wiese Productions, 2011)

Blake Snyder, *Save the Cat!: The Last Book on Screenwriting That You'll Ever Need* (Michael Wiese Productions, 2005)

Constantin Stanislavski, *An Actor Prepares* (Theatre Arts Books, 1936)

Mark Travis, *Directing Feature Films: The Creative Collaboration Between Director, Writers, and Actors* (Michael Wiese Productions, 2002)

John Truby, *The Anatomy of Story: 22 Steps to Becoming a Master Storyteller* (Faber & Faber, 2007)

Christopher Vogler, *The Writer's Journey: Mythic Structure for Writers* (Michael Wiese Productions, 2007)

Judith Weston, *Directing Actors*: *Creating Memorable Performances for Film & Television* (Michael Wiese Productions, 1996)

Charles Wilkinson, *The Working Film Director* (Michael Wiese Productions, 2nd edition, 2013)

ABOUT PETER D. MARSHALL

courtesy Don Chien

Peter D. Marshall is a filmmaker and film-directing coach from Vancouver, Canada. He has worked in the film and television industry for over 40 years — as a film director, television producer, 1st assistant director, and TV series creative consultant.

Peter has directed over 30 episodes of television drama such as *John Woo's Once a Thief*, *Wiseguy*, *21 Jump Street*, *Neon Rider*, *The Black Stallion*, *Scene of the Crime*, *Big Wolf on Campus*, and *Largo Winch*.

As a 1st assistant director, Peter has worked on 12 feature films (including *Dawn of the Dead*, *The Butterfly Effect*, *Happy Gilmore*, and *The Fly II*); 17 television movies; 4 television-series pilots; 7 television series; and over 20 commercials.

He has written, directed, or produced over 50 hours of documentary and educational programs, and his documentaries and dramas have won, or been nominated for, 14 international film awards.

Peter was a directing instructor at the Vancouver Film School for over 8 years, and since 2015 has been the directing instructor and mentor at the Shanghai Vancouver Film School. Peter has also taught film-directing workshops for MediaCorp (Singapore), Raindance Canada, Directors Guild of Canada, Vancouver Institute of Media Arts, Victoria Motion Picture School, Shoreline Actors Lab, and Capilano University.

He has also created and presented filmmaking workshops around the world in places including Canada, China, Malaysia, Haiti, Singapore, and Dubai.

In 1999, Peter created his website, ActionCutPrint.com, and began publishing the free monthly ezine *The Director's Chair*, which is read by filmmakers in over 100 countries. He also has his own filmmaking blog, FilmDirectingTips.com.

THE WRITER'S JOURNEY
3RD EDITION

MYTHIC STRUCTURE FOR WRITERS

CHRISTOPHER VOGLER

BEST SELLER
OVER 170,000 COPIES SOLD!

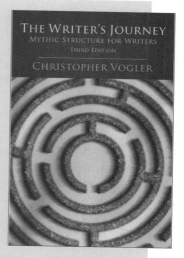

See why this book has become an international best seller and a true classic. *The Writer's Journey* explores the powerful relationship between mythology and storytelling in a clear, concise style that's made it required reading for movie executives, screenwriters, playwrights, scholars, and fans of pop culture all over the world.

Both fiction and nonfiction writers will discover a set of useful myth-inspired storytelling paradigms (i.e., "The Hero's Journey") and step-by-step guidelines to plot and character development. Based on the work of Joseph Campbell, *The Writer's Journey* is a must for all writers interested in further developing their craft.

The updated and revised third edition provides new insights and observations from Vogler's ongoing work on mythology's influence on stories, movies, and man himself.

"This book is like having the smartest person in the story meeting come home with you and whisper what to do in your ear as you write a screenplay. Insight for insight, step for step, Chris Vogler takes us through the process of connecting theme to story and making a script come alive."
> – Lynda Obst, Producer, *Sleepless in Seattle, How to Lose a Guy in 10 Days;*
>   Author, *Hello, He Lied*

"This is a book about the stories we write, and perhaps more importantly, the stories we live. It is the most influential work I have yet encountered on the art, nature, and the very purpose of storytelling."
> – Bruce Joel Rubin, Screenwriter, *Stuart Little 2, Deep Impact,*
>   *Ghost, Jacob's Ladder*

CHRISTOPHER VOGLER is a veteran story consultant for major Hollywood film companies and a respected teacher of filmakers and writers around the globe. He has influenced the stories of movies from *The Lion King* to *Fight Club* to *The Thin Red Line* and most recently wrote the first installment of *Ravenskull*, a Japanese-style manga or graphic novel. He is the executive producer of the feature film *P.S. Your Cat is Dead* and writer of the animated feature *Jester Till*.

$26.95 · 300 PAGES · ORDER NUMBER 76RLS · ISBN: 193290736x

SAVE THE CAT!®
THE LAST BOOK ON SCREENWRITING YOU'LL EVER NEED!

BLAKE SNYDER

BEST SELLER

He's made millions of dollars selling screenplays to Hollywood and now screenwriter Blake Snyder tells all. "Save the Cat!®" is just one of Snyder's many ironclad rules for making your ideas more marketable and your script more satisfying — and saleable, including:
- The four elements of every winning logline.
- The seven immutable laws of screenplay physics.
- The 10 genres and why they're important to your movie.
- Why your Hero must serve your idea.
- Mastering the Beats.
- Mastering the Board to create the Perfect Beast.
- How to get back on track with ironclad and proven rules for script repair.

This ultimate insider's guide reveals the secrets that none dare admit, told by a show biz veteran who's proven that you can sell your script if you can save the cat.

"Imagine what would happen in a town where more writers approached screenwriting the way Blake suggests? My weekend read would dramatically improve, both in sellable/producible content and in discovering new writers who understand the craft of storytelling and can be hired on assignment for ideas we already have in house."
>   – From the Foreword by Sheila Hanahan Taylor, Vice President, Development at Zide/Perry
>   Entertainment, whose films include *American Pie, Cats and Dogs, Final Destination*

"One of the most comprehensive and insightful how-to's out there. Save the Cat!® *is a must-read for both the novice and the professional screenwriter."*
>   – Todd Black, Producer, *The Pursuit of Happyness, The Weather Man, S.W.A.T, Alex and
>   Emma, Antwone Fisher*

"Want to know how to be a successful writer in Hollywood? The answers are here. Blake Snyder has written an insider's book that's informative — and funny, too."
>   – David Hoberman, Producer, *The Shaggy Dog* (2005), *Raising Helen, Walking Tall,
>   Bringing Down the House, Monk* (TV)

BLAKE SNYDER, besides selling million-dollar scripts to both Disney and Spielberg, was one of Hollywood's most successful spec screenwriters. Blake's vision continues on *www.blakesnyder.com.*

$19.95 · 216 PAGES · ORDER NUMBER 34RLS · ISBN: 9781932907001

DIRECTING ACTORS
CREATING MEMORABLE PERFORMANCES
FOR FILM AND TELEVISION

JUDITH WESTON

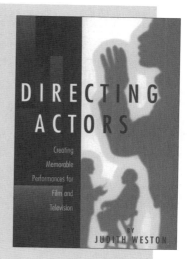

BEST SELLER
OVER 45,000 COPIES SOLD!

Directing film or television is a high-stakes occupation. It captures your full attention at every moment, calling on you to commit every resource and stretch yourself to the limit. It's the white-water rafting of entertainment jobs. But for many directors, the excitement they feel about a new project tightens into anxiety when it comes to working with actors.

This book provides a method for establishing creative, collaborative relationships with actors, getting the most out of rehearsals, troubleshooting poor performances, giving briefer directions, and much more. It addresses what actors want from a director, what directors do wrong, and constructively analyzes the director-actor relationship.

"Judith Weston is an extraordinarily gifted teacher."
— David Chase, Emmy® Award-Winning Writer,
Director, and Producer *The Sopranos,*
Northern Exposure, I'll Fly Away

"I believe that working with Judith's ideas and principles has been the most useful time I've spent preparing for my work. I think that if Judith's book were mandatory reading for all directors, the quality of the director-actor process would be transformed, and better drama would result."
— John Patterson, Director
Six Feet Under, CSI: Crime Scene Investigation,
The Practice, Law and Order

"I know a great teacher when I find one! Everything in this book is brilliant and original and true."
— Polly Platt, Producer, *Bottle Rocket*
Executive Producer, *Broadcast News, The War of the Roses*

JUDITH WESTON was a professional actor for 20 years and has taught Acting for Directors for over a decade.

$26.95 · 314 PAGES · ORDER NUMBER 4RLS · ISBN: 0941188248

THE HOLLYWOOD STANDARD

THE COMPLETE AND AUTHORITATIVE GUIDE TO SCRIPT FORMAT AND STYLE

CHRISTOPHER RILEY

BEST SELLER

Finally, there's a script format guide that is accurate, complete, and easy to use, written by Hollywood's foremost authority on industry standard script formats. Riley's guide is filled with clear, concise, complete instructions and hundreds of examples to take the guesswork out of a multitude of formatting questions that perplex screenwriters, waste their time, and steal their confidence. You'll learn how to get into and out of a POV shot, how to set up a telephone intercut, what to capitalize and why, how to control pacing with format, and more.

"The Hollywood Standard *is not only indispensable, it's practical, readable, and fun to use.*"
— Dean Batali, Writer-Producer, *That '70s Show;* Writer, *Buffy the Vampire Slayer*

"*Buy this book before you write another word! It's required reading for any screenwriter who wants to be taken seriously by Hollywood.*"
— Elizabeth Stephen, President, Mandalay Television Pictures;
Executive Vice President Motion Picture Production, Mandalay Pictures

"*Riley has succeeded in an extremely difficult task: He has produced a guide to screenplay formatting which is both entertaining to read and exceptionally thorough. Riley's clear style, authoritative voice, and well-written examples make this book far more enjoyable than any formatting guide has a right to be. This is the best guide to script formatting ever, and it is an indispensable tool for every writer working in Hollywood.*"
— Wout Thielemans, *Screentalk* Magazine

"*It doesn't matter how great your screenplay is if it looks all wrong.* The Hollywood Standard *is probably the most critical book any screenwriter who is serious about being taken seriously can own. For any writer who truly understands the power of making a good first impression, this comprehensive guide to format and style is priceless.*"
— Marie Jones, *www.absolutewrite.com*

CHRISTOPHER RILEY, based in Los Angeles, developed Warner Brothers Studios script software and serves as the ultimate arbiter of script format for the entertainment industry.

$18.95 · 208 PAGES · ORDER # 31RLS · ISBN: 9781932907018

THE MYTH OF MWP

In a dark time, a light bringer came along, leading the curious and the frustrated to clarity and empowerment. It took the well-guarded secrets out of the hands of the few and made them available to all. It spread a spirit of openness and creative freedom, and built a storehouse of knowledge dedicated to the betterment of the arts.

The essence of the Michael Wiese Productions (MWP) is empowering people who have the burning desire to express themselves creatively. We help them realize their dreams by putting the tools in their hands. We demystify the sometimes secretive worlds of screenwriting, directing, acting, producing, film financing, and other media crafts.

By doing so, we hope to bring forth a realization of 'conscious media' which we define as being positively charged, emphasizing hope and affirming positive values like trust, cooperation, self-empowerment, freedom, and love. Grounded in the deep roots of myth, it aims to be healing both for those who make the art and those who encounter it. It hopes to be transformative for people, opening doors to new possibilities and pulling back veils to reveal hidden worlds.

MWP has built a storehouse of knowledge unequaled in the world, for no other publisher has so many titles on the media arts. Please visit www.mwp.com where you will find many free resources and a 25% discount on our books. Sign up and become part of the wider creative community!

Onward and upward,

Michael Wiese
Publisher/Filmmaker